The Lakeland Peaks

Frontispiece: Striding Edge – Helvellyn

W. A. Poucher, Hon. F.R.P.S.

The Lakeland Peaks

A Pictorial Guide to walking in the district and to the safe ascent of its principal mountain groups with 251 photographs by the author 14 Maps and 142 Routes

Eleventh Edition

For the eleventh edition of this work, any necessary revisions to routes were undertaken by Peter Little

Constable · London

First published in Great Britain 1960
by Constable and Company Ltd
3 The Lanchesters, 162 Fulham Palace Road,
London W6 9ER
Copyright © 1960 by William Arthur Poucher
Second edition 1962
Third edition 1965
Fourth edition 1968
Fifth edition 1971
Sixth edition 1976
Seventh edition 1979
Eighth edition 1981
Ninth edition 1983
Tenth edition 1992
Eleventh edition 1998
ISBN 0 09 77510 9

Set in 9pt Palatino by SetSystems Limited, Saffron Walden, Essex
Printed in Great Britain by
BAS Printers Limited, Over Wallop, Hampshire

Preface to the eleventh edition

The Lakeland Peaks was first published in 1960 and in the years that followed my father made frequent visits to the area in order to see if modifications to any of the routes were required; if so he noted them for inclusion in the next edition. However, in the years before he died he was no longer able to carry out this task, and since his death in 1988 I have not found it possible to do a great deal myself.

Therefore, some time ago, it was agreed with Constable that we should approach someone who knew the Lake District intimately and see if they were prepared to make a survey of all the routes and amend them where necessary. As I had a personal friend who had the necessary qualifications, the publishers agreed that I should contact Peter Little, who I am delighted to say agreed to undertake this work.

Mr Little is an experienced climber and fellwalker who has walked extensively among the Lakeland fells, having climbed most of them many times; he is also a member of the Keswick Mountain Rescue Team. As I think readers will realise after perusing this guide, he was an admirable choice for the task. He has added one new route in the Helvellyn Section – No.78a The Swirls and Browncove Crags – as it is now used by so many walkers. The more technical sections have been revised to conform with current practice and thinking.

In spite of the routes being updated, it is still possible for slight changes to appear due to erosion, rock falls and other natural causes and if such variations are noticed by a user of this guide it will be most helpful if they would let me know so that they can be included in any future edition of this work.

As regular visitors to the area will know, many footpaths had, over the years become so eroded that repair or reinstatement was urgently required. On many hills this work has been carried out; I urge walkers to keep to any such improved or diverted paths in the interests of conservation and, on paths that have not yet been repaired, to walk on the worn part or on stony ground so as not to increase the damage already done.

I would draw readers' attention to a booklet, *Tread Lightly*, produced by the British Mountaineering Council in co-operation with the Mountaineering Council of Scotland, with financial support from the Nature Conservancy Council. This booklet covers many aspects of correct conduct on and around the fells, which is summed up in their phrase: 'Take nothing but photographs, leave nothing but footprints.'

It should be noted that the routes described and illustrated herein have been frequented over the years without objection, but they do not necessarily constitute a right of way. If in any doubt, the reader should contact the owner of the land and ask permission to cross it before embarking upon his walk. This is most important in view of the outbreak of vandalism which has recently swept the country and which has resulted in damage to fences, hedges, gates, walls, cairns and shelters in mountainous districts; this is not only deplorable but also contrary to the accepted Country Code.

Finally, I would urge leaders of school and youth parties not to venture on these hills unless the weather is favourable; moreover, they should always insist upon everyone wearing boots and proper clothing and carrying the various items mentioned in the section devoted to equipment. If they do this they will not only reduce the risk of accidents, but also avoid the, often needless, call for Mountain Rescue.

A route card will be found at the end of the book which is used in Scotland and Snowdonia. This should be completed by all walkers as in the event of an accident it will facilitate Mountain Rescue. However, it is important to complete route cards properly and not to alter routes without notification to the establishment where the original route has been left.

The fourteen maps are reproduced with the permission of John Bartholomew & Son Limited.

John Poucher
Gate Ghyll, High Brigham
Cockermouth, Cumbria
1998

After Mr Poucher's death in August 1988, at the age of 96, his son and daugther-in-law felt that as he had loved the Lake District so much, and had ended his life among its hills and valleys, it would be appropriate for there to be some form of memorial to him in the area. Originally a memorial seat was presented to Woodend Country House, Thornthwaite, where he lived for the last three years of his life. However, as it is now a private residence and the seat has disappeared, permission was obtained from the owner of the Scafell Hotel, Rosthwaite, to site a replacement in its grounds, where it now stands. It bears a plaque which reads:

IN MEMORY OF
WALTER POUCHER 1891–1988
A RENOWNED MOUNTAIN PHOTOGRAPHER
WHO LOVED THE WILD PLACES

Contents

Introductory notes

Lakeland has for many years been one of the most popular holiday centres in Britain because its matchless beauty provides that peaceful environment which appeals to visitors of all ages. When energetic young people first come to the district, they raise their eyes to the peaks and imagine themselves standing by one of the summit cairns inhaling the invigorating mountain air and scanning the valleys far below, the chain of engirdling hills and the distant glimmering sea. Come what may, they lose no time in setting out to climb one of them, and realise their ambition with the satisfaction which comes only after the ardours of the ascent. It is quite probable that they will make Scafell Pike their first conquest, not only because it is the monarch of our English hills, but also because they believe it will reveal the finest and most comprehensive panorama on account of its altitude. Once they have trodden its summit, they quite naturally speculate upon the merits of the views from the other high peaks in the district, and after talking over the question with friends, they will in all probability continue their exploration by climbing Great Gable, Helvellyn, or perhaps even the Old Man of Coniston, on their first holiday.

When these young people return home their thoughts will often revert to these experiences, and especially if they were captivated by the spirit and mystery of the hills. they will doubtless unfold their maps frequently, and by following the routes thereon they will relive these happy experiences. If Scafell Pike was climbed from Borrowdale, their thoughts will follow that grand walk from Seatoller through the delightful terminal stretches of the valley to the hamlet of Seathwaite, the tramp along the stony track to Stockley Bridge with the music of the stream in their ears, the scramble up the shattered slopes to Taylorgill Force with perhaps an inquisitive glance into the wild ravine enclosing it, the ramble up the more gentle declivities of the pass to Sty Head with its sombre tarn on the left, and the impressive crags of the Central Fells visible all the way. They remember that welcome halt for a breather and a chat with other enthusiastic walkers near the cairn, and then on again up the steeper track which suddenly disclosed the glittering waters of Sprinkling Tarn at the foot of the gullied precipices of Great End. Soon after that the shelter at Esk Hause came into view in the dip in the horizon, and when they had reached it, the short walk over to the cairn which revealed another surprise in the Langdale Pikes and the lakes glimmering away in the distance to the south-east. Then followed the high-level tramp along the well-cairned track to Scafell Pike, the traverse of the great boulder-strewn top of Broad Crag, and after crossing the last steep dip in the route, the exhilaration of standing by the huge cairn on the roof of England with a whole kingdom spread out at their feet.

A close inspection of the map will suggest to our friends many other routes to this lofty belvedere, and curiosity will induce them to ponder over their respective merits. Would the Corridor Route have been more interesting? Perhaps it would have been a greater thrill to have stayed in Wasdale and to have ascended the mountain by way of Mickeldore, or what about the approaches from Eskdale via Cam Spout? Then another line of thought will probably develop, for they had seen a grand array of peaks engirdling the horizon from the Pike and they will now speculate again upon the merits of the panoramas from their summits, to realise quite suddenly that a lifetime is not too long in which to become acquainted with them all.

Their cogitations will follow a normal course and they will do exactly the same as the rest of us did in our novitiate, for they will formulate plans for their next vacation long before it is due. Next time, they decide, they will stay in another valley and explore the adjacent hills; but which one, and which hills?

To solve this problem they will often lay their map on the table, and while scanning it with joyful anticipation will also study the various guide books which describe this enchanting country. There they will read what their authors have so lucidly written, but much will inevitably be left to their imagination.

It is here that my long experience of the Lakeland Peaks will help them to resolve these difficulties, for by consulting this volume (in conjuncton with my other works devoted to this district) they will not only be able to choose their centre with certainty, their routes to the peaks in the vicinity in accordance with their powers as walkers, and their subjects for the camera if they happen to be photographers, but they will also be able to *see* beforehand through the medium of my camera studies precisely the type of country that will satisfy every one of their personal tastes.

The following Ordnance Survey maps are available to visitors to the area:

1:50 000   Landranger: Sheets 89 West Cumbria; 90 Penrith & Keswick; 96 Barrow in Furness & South Lakeland Area; 97 Kendal to Morecambe.

1:25 000   Outdoor Leisure (The English Lakes): Nos. 4 North Western Area; 5 North Eastern Area; 6 South Western Area and 7 South Eastern Area.

The one inch to one mile Touring Map and Guide 3, The Lake District, is also worth considering; although the scale is not metric, the heights are shown in metres and it does cover the whole area on one sheet.

There is also Bartholomew's Lake District Walking Map, at a scale of one inch to one mile. Although it still shows heights in feet, with contour intervals of 250 feet, its layer system of colouring, and the fact that it covers the whole area on a single sheet, may be attractive to some walkers.

Equipment

Anyone who ventures on to the hills without being properly equipped is foolhardy. The weather in the mountains can change rapidly and even in the summer extremes of cold and heat may be encountered whilst out in the hills.

Footwear is of paramount importance. There are a number of considerations to be borne in mind when making a choice from the vast array of walking and climbing boots available. Cost is obviously important and it usually follows that the more expensive boots are likely to provide the wearer with longer use and greater comfort.

Walking boots must be sturdy and have a good sole. There are a variety of styles available in addition to the classic Vibram pattern. Some lay claim to a host of uses in all terrains and in truth there are few that don't match up to their sales hype. Be wary though of plastic soles on the cheaper models or those that are notoriously slippery when used on wet rocks and grass.

There are two main types of upper available. The most satisfactory for longevity is without doubt leather. Carefully looked after and kept clean and well dubbined, leather can be perfectly weather-repellent. The more seams, and therefore stitching, there are in a boot, the more difficult it is to trust its waterproofing. Water will find its way through even the tiniest of weaknesses and often the problem will not be the boot itself but the fact that water gets in through the top and the gaps along the lacing system.

There are numerous models made with tough nylon uppers. Material such as Cordura is particularly hardwearing. Often, and certainly in the case of the more expensive varieties, they will include a breathable lining such as Goretex. Many boots

Plate 1

Plate 2

constructed in this way claim impressive water-repellent properties, but over a period of long and hard use these dwindle considerably.

Proprietary cleaners and reproofing substances are required from time to time to increase the life of such footwear. There is a need to tread somewhat more carefully over sharp rocks as the material is easily damaged. This type of footwear is generally unsuited to walking in snowy conditions for it does not provide sufficient warmth or the rigidity required to kick steps and use crampons successfully.

For those who might go scrambling along airy ridges and buttresses or rock climbing on cliff and crag, a more rigid boot may be found more suitable for tiptoeing on tiny edges. Such boots will differ from walking boots in that they will have a stiffener inside the sole lending varying degrees of rigidity. A three-quarter stiffener is perhaps the most versatile all round and a full shank for total stiffness might be needed by the ice climber.

Readers will no doubt encounter plastic mountaineering boots. Normally these are for serious mountaineering in harsh winter conditions in the Alps and the highest mountains of the world. For the fellwalker they are totally unsuitable, being cumbersome, over-warm, and harsh on feet and knees.

Be sure to take good care of your feet at all times. Many modern boots require little or no breaking-in period. For those that do, make sure that at the first sign of any soreness you cover that part of your foot with plaster to prevent the formation of blisters. A stoical attitude in the face of soreness is foolish because it may mean curtailment of a long-planned holiday.

Waterproof clothing is an essential requirment for all who go into the hills. Being wet will turn a great day into one of continual misery and, worse, may lead to hypothermia and the necessity for rescue. Nowadays there is little excuse for not having at least reasonably good waterproof or shell clothing, for there is a wide choice not simply in mountaineering shops but also in the high street. It does follow however that the best shell clothing for the job is generally to be found in specialist shops. There are a variety of waterproof but breathable materials that serve the fellwalker admirably. Cheaper garments made from proofed nylon in varying weights are perfectly adequate for mountain wear and suffer only from the problem of condensation build-up on the inside of the garment. This may lead to a little discomfort and dampness but provided that the shell is worn at all times there will be no chilling effect from the wind.

Any good waterproof jacket should be well cut and allow freedom of movement. A large and accommodating hood is a good idea, and one that closes snugly around the face but doesn't restrict vision is preferable. Such hoods will normally have a wired or at least stiffened visor. Pockets should be easily accessible whilst you are wearing a rucksack hip belt, and a large pocket to take a map is a worthwhile addition. Some jackets feature zipped underarm air vents. These are very useful in steamy conditions, when it is wet but warm. The sleeve closures must be convenient and it is a good idea to check that they can be easily done up with gloved hands. A full-length zip that operates in two directions is useful in that it provides good ventilation. A storm flap inside the zip will make it more weathertight. The alternative to a jacket is a pull-over-the-head anorak or cagoule. This type of shell is clearly a more stormproof garment but lacks the ability to ventilate efficiently. At the end of the day it is largely a matter of personal choice and how deep into one's pocket one has to delve.

Many people comment on how unnecessary a pair of waterproof trousers is. One can only assume that such people have never spent time in the mountains in really wild weather. A large proportion of body heat is lost through the thighs, and once they are wet this loss is exaggerated considerably. Over-trousers are essential for comfort and well-being. When choosing a pair, ensure that you are able to get them on over the top of your walking boots. It's a good idea to buy a pair with a short knee-length zip that facilitates this, and it is possible to buy trousers with a full-length zip that allows the wearer to put them on and take them off more easily. Trousers with a 'drop seat' are convenient for a number of good reasons.

Fleece clothing is well established as an efficient insulator. A wide range of products is available and the prospective purchaser usually has a large choice of differing weights and a bewildering array of patterns and colours. Fleece has a tremendous advantage over more traditional insulation, such as wool, in that it retains warmth even when wet and dries out very quickly. It is not, however, windproof and can only be made so by additional shell clothing or, as is more popular, by a Pertex covering. Jackets, jumpers and trousers are all available in fleece from all the top manufacturers.

Breeches are rarely seen these days having been largely superseded by a range of cotton/polyester trousers. Light-weight but very durable and often windproof, these are a rather more sensible alternative. For colder weather long johns can be worn underneath or it may be preferable to resort to wearing fleece trousers when conditions become extremely cold.

Microfibre undergarments are a worthwhile addition to the winter wardrobe and may even be required at other times of the year. To achieve the most from such garments they should ideally be worn next to the skin and be quite a snug fit.

Gloves or mitts ought to be carried on all but the most reliable of summer days. Again there is tremendous choice from the cheapest to the most outrageously expensive. Fleece gloves or mitts are useful for the same reason as previously mentioned but you might consider a windproof outer worhtwhile. Gloves made from waterproof breathable fabrics are only of any use if the material is fairly heavy. Woollen mitts such as the eternal Dachstein are particularly warm even when wet or completely frozen – unfortunately it is difficult to hold things with any security when wearing them. It is worth considering wearing a lighter weight inner glove which can be used on its own in all but the coldest conditions.

Hats and balaclavas are also a necessity. Here once again fleece is an efficient insulator. An outer covering of breathable waterproof material makes a hat both windproof and water-resistant. Traditional woolly bobble hats are fine and so also is the mountaineer's balaclava which folds up into a hat when you no longer need full head protection.

Gaiters are a covering for the lower part of the leg. Essentially they are worn to prevent snow from getting into the top of the boot, melting and causing wet uncomfortable feet. They are equally suitable for use in the rain, and when overtrousers are worn they will stop water percolating down the leg into the top of the boot. Ordinary proofed nylon or waterproof breath-able models are available.

A rucksack will be needed to carry food and spare clothing. There is perhaps more choice available in rucksacks than any other single item of mountaineering equipment for in addition to the more well established marques there are a huge number of cheaper makes.

A rucksack for day use need not be too large. There is a saying among mountain folk that no matter what size sack you have you will nearly always fill it. That's no good at all if you have a 60 litre sack on a day trip. Normally something around 25 to 30 litres will be more than adequate. In this size, the range is perhaps largest and the final choice must be left to the individual purchaser. Few rucksacks are waterproof though some claim to be, and it is usually necessary to place items in a polythene bag inside the pack. Outside pockets are useful for storing things to which quick access is required, particularly water bottles on hot days; if your chosen rucksack has a lid it is likely to have an integral pocket.

A compass is another essential piece of equipment. The Silva compass is by far and away the most common though there are other makes. Whichever compass you choose it should have a large base plate which enables you to measure long distances on the map. More about the compass and map will be found in the chapter on navigation.

A whistle, emergency bivvy bag, head torch and first aid kit will complete the basic equipment required for safe travel in our hills; these can be supplemented with safety equipment necessary for winter walking or for scrambling and rock climbing.

List of equipment for summer hill walking
Boots
Waterproof shell clothing: jacket and trousers
Fleece jumper and spare (wool is an alternative)
Warm hat and gloves or mitts
Cotton trousers or breeches with long socks
Some food and emergency food
A flask or, if it is a hot summer day, a water bottle
Map and compass
Whistle
Emergency bivvy bag
Small first aid kit
Gaiters
Head torch.

Winter supplement
Warm undergarments
Spare mitts or gloves
Lightweight insulated jacket or waistcoat
Balaclava
Ice axe and crampons

Rock climbing

The Lakeland Peaks afford ample opportunities for the enjoyment of this exhilarating sport, but a novice should never attempt it without guidance and training. If you have a friend who is an experienced rock climber, ask him to tell you about its technique and the management of the rope, and at the first opportunity get him to lead you up some of the easy routes, when you will have the chance to put these theories into practice. If you have a steady head, good balance and can acquire the rhythm required for proficiency, he will soon notice it and lead you up routes of greater difficulty until finally you tackle the severes.

In the event of your becoming keen on rock climbing, you might wish to apply for membership of one of the climbing clubs of which the Fell and Rock is the acknowledged leader in the English Lake District. But owing to the great popularity of this sport this well known club, like many others in Britain, is so full that additional members are strictly limited at present. This club issues a series of comprehensive Climbing Guides which contain precise details of every known route of importance in the district.

The Lakeland centres

In the following list I have given the principal centres from which the Lakeland Peaks may be most conveniently climbed. But it should be borne in mind that strong walkers are often able to reach them from more distant centres, such as Youth Hostels, which are sometimes less conveniently situated. At the time of writing there were twenty-eight Hostels listed in the Lake District section of the YHA Accommodation Guide. I have only cited those giving ready access to the major hill ranges.

Wasdale is the best centre in the district for rock climbing and is ideally situated for the routes on Scafell, Gable and Pillar. In view of its importance the accommodation available is much too limited, and apart from the Wasdale Head Inn and Brackenclose, the latter belonging to the Fell and Rock Climbing Club, there are only four farmsteads. Burnthwaite stands in the shadow of Great Gable at the foot of Sty Head; Wasdale Head Hall is just off the Burnmoor track at the head of Wastwater; and Middle Fell and Rowhead farms are on the Black Sail side of the inn. There is a Youth Hostel at Wasdale Hall, facing the Screes at the foot of Wastwater.

Ennerdale has very limited accommodation apart from its two Youth Hostels, one at Gillerthwaite Farm, about one mile east of the head of the lake, and the other, Black Sail, at the head of the dale, which is perfectly situated for the ascents of Pillar, Gable, Haystacks and High Stile. A bed may also be found at one of the local farms.

Buttermere is a favourite Lakeland centre and very convenient for climbing High Stile, Dale Head and Grasmoor, but Gable and Pillar are only within the range of strong walkers. This enchanting valley is resplendent with hotels and farms, from any of which the above ascents may be made as well as the circuit of either Buttermere or Crummock Water. Scale Hill and Loweswater are more distant, but make excellent centres for the ascent of Mellbreak and the Grasmoor group of hills. There are Youth Hostels both at Buttermere and on Honister Hause.

Newlands is well situated for the Grasmoor and Dale Head groups and numerous beds are available at the farms in the valley. The Youth Hostels at Keswick and Longthwaite give easy access to this neighbourhood.

Keswick brings many of the groups of hills within range by car, cycle or bus. It is perfectly situated for the ascent of Skiddaw and for the walk round Derwentwater, whilst Bassenthwaite, Blencathra, the Watendlath Fells and the High Spy–Cat Bells section of the Dale Head group are not too far away for the average walker. There is a Youth Hostel in Station Road in the town and another at Skiddaw House, in wild country on the Cumbrian Way east of Skiddaw.

Borrowdale is undoubtedly one of the best centres in all Lakeland; not only is it well provided with hotels and every other type of accommodation, but it is also admirably situated for the ascents of Dale Head, Haystacks, Great Gable, Glaramara, Great End, Scafell Pike and Bowfell; even the Langdale Pikes are within range of a strong walker. Add to all these the accessibility of the Watendlath Fells and you have the cream of the Lakeland Peaks within reach of the energetic walker. There is a Youth Hostel at Longthwaite in a marvellous woodland setting near Rosthwaite and another at Barrow House near Grange.

Patterdale has plenty of accommodation throughout the valley from Glenridding to Brothers Water and Low Hartsop, comprising hotels, guest houses and farms of all types. In addition to the lovely scenes round Ullswater it is the best base for the ascents of Helvellyn and Fairfield, and a good one for High Street. Howtown is also well situated for the last-named range of hills, as well as for the lower reaches of the lake. There are Youth Hostels at Goldrill House, Patterdale and at Greenside, Glenridding, while the Fell and Rock Climbing club have a splendid hut near Brothers Water.

Mardale has very little accommodation apart from the comfortable Haweswater Hotel, unless the farms towards Bampton are patronised. It is admirably placed for the ascents of High Street and Harter Fell, whilst the Shap Fells are also within reach.

Long Sleddale, Kentmere and Troutbeck are extensive valleys with a variety of accommodation, and the farmsteads at their heads are in close proximity to the High Street and Ill Bell ranges. Those situated in the last-named valley are convenient for the ascent of Wansfell and for the walks round the upper reaches of Windermere. The nearest Youth Hostels are in Ambleside and Kendal.

Ambleside and Grasmere are splendid centres for those using a car, cycle or bus for transport to the more distant hills. Without such conveniences the walker is restricted to the Helvellyn range, Wansfell, Loughrigg, Silver How, the Langdale Pikes, Helm Crag and the low hills about Easedale. Both places have plenty of accommodation to suit all tastes and are within reach of all the adjacent lakes and tarns. There are Youth Hostels at Ambleside, two in Grasmere and another at High Grove, Loughrigg.

Langdale has ample accommodation from Skelwith Bridge and Elterwater right up to the Old Hotel at the head of the valley. Their situation is perfect for the ascents of the Langdale Pikes and Bowfell, while even the Coniston Fells, Scafell Pike and Gable may be visited by strong walkers. There is a Youth Hostel at Elterwater and members of the Fell and Rock Climbing Club have accommodation at Raw Head Farm. At the New Dungeon Ghyll Hotel, the development of Sticklebarn to include a bar, self-service licensed grillroom and cafeteria specifically designed for the needs of walkers and climbers, in any weather, was most welcome.

Coniston has numerous hotels and guest houses, while farms are dotted about in nearby valleys. These are well placed for access to the Consiton Fells, Tarn Hows and Hawkshead, to say nothing of the many adjacent lakes. There are two Youth Hostels in Coniston and one at Esthwaite Lodge, Hawkshead.

Dunnerdale is rather too distant for access to the higher hills in the district, save the Coniston group and Harter Fell, Eskdale. There is an inn at Seathwaite, and numerous farms as high up the dale as Cockley Beck.

Eskdale is a splendid base for the Scafell and Bowfell ranges and affords one of the finest approaches to them both. Eskdale Green and Boot have a fair amount of accommodation, the Woolpack Inn being the highest hotel in the valley, and Taw House and Brotherilkeld its two most remote farmsteads. Hard Knott and Harter Fell are easily reached from them all, but the two main groups involve a long day on the hills. There is a Youth Hostel at Boot.

Cockermouth, a pleasant market town in the west of the region, is less crowded in the holiday season than those centres in the heart of Lakeland. There is ample accommodation to be found in its many hotels and there is a Youth Hostel at Double Mills, just to the south of the town. With transport, it is a good base for outings to the Buttermere, Loweswater, Newlands and Borrowdale areas, and if more lengthy drives are contemplated, then Ennerdale, Wasdale, Eskdale and even Dunnerdale are within reach.

Note: For those who wish to look after themselves there is a large variety of self-catering accommodation available, and also campsites and caravan parks, throughout the district.

The Lakeland Peaks
142 Routes of ascent

The Scafell Group Map 1

SCAFELL PIKE

SCAFELL

GREAT END

LINGMELL

The Gable Group Map 2

GREAT GABLE

The High Stile Group Map 4
46 Buttermere and Scale Force
47 Buttermere and Far Ruddy Beck
48 Buttermere and Sourmilk Gill
49 Buttermere and Burtness (Birkness) Comb
50 Buttermere and Scarth Gap
51 Warnscale Bottom and Haystacks
52 Honister Hause and Haystacks
53 Gillerthwaite and Red Pike
54 Ennerdale and Starling Dodd

The Dale Head Group Map 5
55 Rosthwaite and Dalehead Tarn
56 Honister direct
57 Buttermere and Robinson
58 Newlands and Robinson
59 Newlands and Hindscarth
60 Newlands Beck and Dalehead Tarn
61 Keswick and Cat Bells
62 Grange and Castle Crag

The Grasmoor Group Map 6
63 Braithwaite and Grisedale Pike
64 Stair and Causey Pike
65 Buttermere and Wandope
66 Lanthwaite Green and Gasgale Gill
67 Whiteside and Hopegill Head

Skiddaw and Blencathra Map 7
SKIDDAW
68 Latrigg and Jenkin Hill
69 Millbeck and Carl Side

BLENCATHRA
70 Scales and Sharp Edge
71 Threlkeld and Hall's Fell

HIGH STREET, SOUTH Map 11
  98 Kentmere and Nan Bield Pass
  99 Troutbeck and Ill Bell
 100 Troutbeck and Thornthwaite Crag

HARTER FELL, MARDALE
 101 From Nan Bield Pass
 102 Mardale and Gatescarth Pass
 103 Long Sleddale and Gatescarth Pass

The Langdale Pikes Map 12
 104 By Stickle Ghyll
 105 By Pavey Ark
 106 By Dungeon Ghyll and Pike o'Stickle
 107 Mickleden and Stake Pass
 108 Rosthwaite and Stake Pass
 109 Greenup Gill and High Raise
 110 Dock Tarn and Ullscarf
 111 Wythburn and Greenup Edge
 112 Grasmere and Far Easedale
 113 By Easedale Tarn
 114 By Silver How

The Bowfell Group Map 13
BOWFELL
 115 Esk Hause and Esk Pike
 116 Rossett Gill and Ore Gap
 117 By The Band direct
 118 By The Band and Three Tarns
 119 Brotherilkeld and Lingcove Beck

CRINKLE CRAGS
 120 From Three Tarns
 121 By Hell Gill
 122 By Crinkle Gill

Heights of the Peaks
in metres and feet

1	978	3209	Scafell Pike
2	964	3163	Scafell
3	950	3117	Helvellyn
4	931	3054	Skiddaw
5	925	3035	Lower Man (Helvellyn)
6	910	2985	Great End
7	902	2959	Bowfell
8	899	2949	Great Gable
9	892	2926	Pillar
10	891	2923	Nethermost Pike
11	890	2920	Catstye Cam
12	885	2903	Esk Pike
13	883	2897	Raise (Helvellyn)
14	873	2864	Fairfield
15	868	2847	Blencathra
16	865	2838	Little Man (Skiddaw)
17	863	2831	White Side (Helvellyn)
18	859	2818	Crinkle Crags (Long Top)
19	858	2815	Dollywaggon Pike
20	857	2812	Great Dodd
21	852	2795	Grasmoor
22	843	2766	Stybarrow Dodd
23	841	2759	Scoat Fell
24	841	2759	St Sunday Crag
25	839	2752	Crag Hill (Eel Crag)
26	828	2716	High Street
27	826	2710	Red Pike (Wasdale)
28	822	2697	Hart Crag
29	819	2687	Steeple
30	815	2674	Shelter Crags
31	807	2648	High Stile

32	807	2648	Lingmell
33	803	2634	Coniston Old Man
34	802	2631	High Raise (High Street)
35	802	2631	Kirk Fell
36	802	2631	Swirl How
37	801	2628	Green Gable
38	797	2615	Haycock
39	796	2611	Brim Fell
40	792	2598	Dove Crag
41	791	2595	Grisedale Pike
42	785	2575	Allen Crags
43	785	2575	Great Carrs
44	784	2572	Thornthwaite Crag
45	783	2569	Glaramara
46	c780	2559	Kidsty Pike
47	778	2552	Dow Crag
48	778	2552	Harter Fell (Mardale)
49	776	2546	Red Screes
50	c773	2536	Grey Friar
51	773	2536	Sail
52	772	2533	Wandope
53	770	2526	Hopegill Head (Hobcarton Pike)
54	763	2503	Stony Cove Pike (Caudale Moor)
55	762	2500	High Raise (Langdale)
56	762	2500	Slight Side
57	762	2500	Wetherlam
58	760	2493	Mardale Ill Bell
59	757	2483	Ill Bell
60	755	2477	Red Pike (Buttermere)
61	753	2470	Dale Head
62	746	2447	Carl Side
63	744	2441	High Crag
64	737	2418	Robinson
65	736	2415	Harrison Stickle
66	736	2415	Seat Sandal

67	727	2385	Hindscarth
68	726	2382	Clough Head
69	726	2382	Ullscarf
70	720	2362	Froswick
71	719	2359	Whiteside (Grasmoor)
72	718	2356	Birkhouse Moor
73	715	2346	Brandreth
74	713	2339	Branstree
75	709	2326	Pike o'Stickle
76	706	2316	Yoke
77	705	2313	Pike o'Blisco
78	702	2303	Bowscale Fell
79	701	2300	Cold Pike
80	c700	2296	Pavey Ark
81	c697	2287	Caw Fell
82	697	2287	Grey Knotts
83	692	2270	Seatallen
84	690	2264	Great Calva
85	c673	2208	Wether Hill
86	672	2205	Scar Crags
87	c663	2175	Carrock Fell
88	660	2165	Whiteless Pike
89	657	2155	Place Fell
90	656	2152	High Pike (Scandale Fell)
91	653	2142	Harter Fell (Eskdale)
92	653	2142	High Spy
93	648	2126	Fleetwith Pike
94	646	2119	Base Brown
95	637	2090	Causey Pike
96	633	2077	Starling Dodd
97	628	2060	Yewbarrow
98	627	2057	Looking Stead (Pillar)
99	621	2037	Walna Scar
100	616	2021	Great Borne
101	609	1998	Illgill Head

102	600	1968	Black Combe
103	597	1959	Haystacks
104	576	1890	Maiden Moor
105	567	1860	Angletarn Pikes
106	553	1814	Steel Fell
107	535	1755	Whin Rigg
108	522	1712	Border End
109	512	1680	Mellbreak
110	488	1601	Grike
111	484	1588	Wansfell
112	451	1480	Cat Bells
113	405	1329	Helm Crag
114	395	1296	Silver How
115	368	1207	Latrigg
116	335	1099	Loughrigg Fell

c No 'Spot Height' shown, so summit height calculated from contours.

Heights of the Passes
in metres and feet

1	759	2490	Esk Hause
2	738	2420	Sticks Pass
3	640	2100	Nan Bield Pass
4	610	2001	Coledale Hause
5	608	1995	Greenup Edge
6	606	1990	Walna Scar Pass
7	594	1950	Gatescarth pass
8	588	1929	Grisedale Hause
9	549	1800	Black Sail Pass
10	512	1680	Scandale Pass
11	488	1600	Sty Head Pass
12	480	1576	Stake Pass
13	455	1492	Kirkstone Pass
14	442	1450	Garburn Pass
15	427	1400	Scarth Gap
16	396	1300	Floutern Tarn
17	393	1290	Hardknott Pass
18	393	1290	Wrynose Pass
19	363	1190	Honister Hause
20	333	1093	Newlands Hause
21	318	1043	Whinlatter Pass
22	274	900	Burnmoor
23	238	782	Dunmail Raise
24	159	523	Red Bank

Heights above OD of the Lakes and Tarns
in metres and feet

1	718	2356	Red Tarn (Helvellyn)
2	713	2340	Three Tarns
3	597	1960	Sprinkling Tarn
4	596	1955	Greycrag Tarn
5	594	1949	Scoat Tarn
6	579	1900	Scales Tarn
7	561	1842	Blind Tarn
8	549	1800	Angle Tarn (Rossett)
9	544	1786	Low Water (Coniston)
10	537	1763	Grisedale Tarn
11	530	1739	Red Tarn (Crinkles)
12	518	1700	Bleaberry Tarn
13	503	1650	Dalehead Tarn
14	503	1650	Innominate Tarn (Haystacks)
15	502	1646	Goat's Water
16	488	1600	Angle Tarn (Patterdale)
17	488	1600	Low Tarn (Wasdale)
18	488	1600	Tarn at Leaves
19	484	1588	Blea Water
20	481	1580	Blackbeck Tarn
21	476	1562	Blea Tarn (Watendlath)
22	469	1540	Stickle Tarn
23	466	1528	Codale Tarn
24	452	1484	Small Water
25	436	1430	Sty Head Tarn
26	421	1383	Hayeswater
27	411	1350	Levers Water
28	403	1322	Dock Tarn
29	402	1320	Greendale Tarn
30	396	1300	Lingmoor Tarn
31	381	1250	Floutern Tarn
32	375	1230	Seathwaite Reservoir
33	366	1200	Alcock Tarn

34	310	1017	Skeggles Water
35	305	1000	Stony Tarn
36	299	980	Greenburn Tarn
37	296	973	Kentmere Reservoir
38	289	950	Gurnal Dubs (Potter Fell)
39	279	915	Easedale Tarn
40	259	850	Harrop Tarn
41	258	847	Watendlath Tarn
42	253	832	Burnmoor Tarn
43	241	790	Haweswater
44	233	766	Devoke Water
45	221	724	Siney Tarn
46	213	700	Blea Tarn (Boot)
47	213	700	Eel Tarn (Woolpack Inn)
48	188	617	Tarn Hows
49	186	612	Blea Tarn (Langdale)
50	176	578	Thirlmere
51	163	536	Beacon Tarn
52	158	520	Brothers Water
53	145	476	Ullswater
54	121	397	Loweswater
55	112	368	Ennerdale Water
56	104	340	Little Langdale Tarn
57	100	329	Buttermere
58	98	321	Crummock Water
59	94	308	Loughrigg Tarn
60	74	244	Derwentwater
61	68	223	Bassenthwaite Lake
62	66	217	Esthwaite Water
63	62	204	Grasmere
64	61	200	Wastwater
65	57	187	Elterwater
66	55	181	Rydal Water
67	43	143	Coniston Water
68	42	138	Blelham Tarn
69	40	130	Windermere

Mountain photography

I have already written and lectured extensively on this fascinating branch of photography, and in both my *Lakeland Through the Lens* and *Climbing with a Camera – The Lake District* I included notes on its application to the mountains of this region.

However, since both these works have been out of print for many years, it may be useful to give a summary of the essentials here for the benefit of the many walkers who are also keen photographers wishing to improve the results they obtain, both in black and white and in colour, in the atmospheric conditions that they will encounter in Lakeland.

1 **The ideal camera for the mountaineer** is undoubtedly the modern miniature owing to its compact form, quick manipulation, great depth of focus, variable zoom lenses and lightness in weight. While these instruments are represented in their very best and most expensive type by the Leica, Pentax and Nikon series, it does not follow that other less costly makes will not give good photographs. Many of these cheaper cameras will give perfectly good results for those who require their camera to provide them with pictures of the most poignant moments of their holiday. The great joy of such equipment is that it is foolproof in use and so long as you remember to keep your finger away from the lens you will have good pictures. For the more discerning photographers, those who require greater flexibility in choosing aperture and shutter speed, an SLR camera with a zoom lens or a variety of fixed focus lenses is essential. Here too it is possible to obtain fully automated cameras that require little more than a point and click technique – even the winding on of the film frame is done for you. However, such cameras are heavily reliant on battery power and in the event of battery failure may not work at all.

2 **The lens** is the most important feature and the best of them naturally facilitate the perfect rendering of the subject. A wide aperture is not essential, because it is seldom necessary to work out of doors at anything greater than F/4.5. It is advisable to use the objective at infinity in mountain photography because overall sharpness is then obtained, and to stop down where required to bring the foreground into focus. It is in this connection that the cheaper camera, which of course is fitted with an inexpensive lens, falls short of its more costly competitors; for the latter are corrected for every known fault and the resulting photographs are then not only more acceptable for enlarged reproduction but also yield exhibition prints of superlative quality. Three lenses are desirable in this branch of photography: 1. a 28 mm or 35 mm wide angle; 2. a standard 50 mm which is usually supplied with most cameras; and 3. a long focus lens such as a 135 mm or even a 200 mm. These cover every likely requirement: the wide angle is most useful when on a mountain or lofty ridge; the 50 mm encompasses the average scene, such as hill and valley; and the long focus is an advantage when the subject is very distant. An analysis of their use in the photographs in this book is as follows:

Wide angle 45 per cent

Standard 50 per cent

Long focus 5 per cent

It is possible to obtain extremely high quality zoom lenses that incorporate all of the above focal lengths. This is quite obviously an advantage in that it not only means carrying less weight and bulk but also facilitates the accurate framing of the picture without having to change lenses.

3 **A lens hood** is an indispensable accessory, because it cuts out adventitious light and increases the brilliance and clarity of the picture. Many people have the illusion that this gadget is only required when the sun is shining and that it is used to keep the direct rays out of the lens when facing the light

source. While its use is then imperative, they often overlook the fact that light is reflected from many points of the hemisphere around the optical axis, and it is the interception of this incidental light that is important.

4 **A filter** is desirable, especially for the good rendering of skyscapes. For black and white photography a pale orange yields the most dramatic results, providing there are not vast areas of trees in the landscape in which all detail would be lost. It is safer to use a yellow filter, which does not suffer from this defect, and with autumn colours a green filter is very effective. The exposure factors do not differ materially, and in view of the wide latitude of modern black and white film the resulting slight differences in density can be corrected when printing.

For colour work a skylight filter is essential for reducing the intensity of the blues and for eliminating haze. Many people also like to use a polarising filter which can enhance a picture by making light waves vibrate in a single plane. This is particularly useful when there is light from many directions such as reflections off water, or more obviously, from snow.

5 **The choice of film** is wide. For straightforward colour print photography a film with an ASA rating of 100 will be sufficient for almost everything you need. For more dreary light, faster speeds up to 400ASA may be useful. Transparency, or slide, film yields excellent results and there is again a wide choice. Some films such as Kodachrome or Fujichrome include processing in the price whereas there are others that do not. Processing for such films is by the E6 process and if this is your chosen medium you should try to find a company that produces excellent results, for they do vary.

Black and white film is available in similar ratings; those that work with this medium will appreciate the subtleties that it offers both in the latitude of the film and in the creation of pictures in the dark-room.

Plate 3 The Scafell Pikes from Border End

A basic point to remember about any film is that the faster the ASA rating the more 'grainy' a picture becomes. Though this factor will not be noticeable on a small scale, it will become all too apparent the more the picture is enlarged.

6 **Exposure** is important when taking a picture but is not relevant to those cameras where the photographer has no control over the aperture and shutter speed.

A slow shutter speed will necessitate holding the camera very steady. If you are using a long or heavy lens it may be preferable to put it on a tripod. A fast shutter speed will capture images and freeze them even though the object may be moving. A minimum shutter speed of 125/sec is a yardstick from which to work.

The aperture determines how much of the scene will be in focus. The smaller the aperture used, the larger the area of the picture that will be in focus. If you are taking pictures of far-away scenes it is not so important to consider the aperture. If, however, you would like to take a picture that includes some close foreground detail, such as your companion, you will require a greater depth of focus and a smaller aperture will be necessary (in photographic terms this is called depth of field). An aperture of F/8 is a versatile minimum with which to work.

The more successful pictures are the result of a carefully considered combination of shutter speed and aperture.

7 **The best time of year** for photography among the Lakeland Peaks is the month of May. A limpid atmosphere and fine cumulus are then a common occurrence and less time is wasted in waiting for suitable lighting. Colour work at this time is also satisfactory because the landscape still reveals the reds of the dead bracken, which, however, disappear in June with the rapid growth of the new fresh green fronds.

Nevertheless, the most dramatic colour transparencies are obtained during the last week of October because the newly dead bracken is then a fiery red, the grass has turned to golden yellow, and the longer shadows increase the contrast between peak and valley.

8 **Lack of sharpness** is a problem that causes disappointment and, although one is often apt to blame the lens, this defect is generally caused by camera shake. It is one thing to hold the instrument steady at ground level with a good stance and no strong wind to disturb the balance, while it is quite another problem in the boisterous breezes on the lofty ridges of Lakeland. When these conditions prevail, it is risky to use a slow shutter speed, and maximum stability may be achieved by leaning against a slab of rock or in a terrific gale of wind by even lying down and jamming the elbows into the space between the crags; but foreground should never be sacrificed on this account. In calm weather a light tripod may be used, but in all other conditions it is too risky to erect one and have it blown over a precipice!

9 **Lighting** is the key to fine mountain photography, and the sun at an angle of 45 degrees, over the left or right shoulder, will yield the required contrasts. These conditions usually appertain in the early morning or late evening. If possible avoid exposures at midday with the sun overhead when the lighting is flat and uninteresting. Before starting on any outing, study the topography of your mountain so that full advantage can be taken of the lighting. Moreover, never be persuaded to discard your camera when setting out in bad weather; the atmosphere in the hills is subject to the most sudden and unexpected changes, and sometimes wet mornings develop into fine afternoons, with magnificent clouds and limpid lighting. If your camera is then away back in your lodgings, you may live to regret the omission!

10 **The sky** is often the saving feature in mountain photographs, since cloudless conditions or a sunless landscape

seldom yield a pleasing picture. Fine sailing white cumulus are always a welcome crown to any mountain scene, and often last a full morning which allows ample time to reach a selected viewpoint for a favourite subject. But really dramatic skies, with fast-moving cloud shadows, are rare and can develop so rapidly that it is a matter of luck if you are near a superb viewpoint you know and from which you can capture the whole scene at its best. Such conditions prevailed in upper Eskdale, dominated by the Scafell Pikes, as portrayed in Plate 3, which was taken from Border End above Hardknott Pass, a belvedere that is perhaps the finest in all Lakeland. Readers of some of my earlier art volumes will have seen the same shot with cloudless skies and even in mist, but this one, exposed about 4 p.m. on a perfect afternoon in late October, is the finest in my collection. A coloured version in Kodachrome appears on pages 186/187 in *The Best of Poucher's Lakeland*, published in 1997.

11 **Haze** is one of the bugbears in this branch of photography, and these conditions are especially prevelent among the Lakeland Peaks during July and August. If an opalescent effect is desired, this is the time of year to secure it, but while such camera studies may be favoured by the purist, they seldom appeal to mountaineers who prefer to see the detail they know exists in their subjects.

12 **Design or composition** is the most outstanding feature of a good camera study; that is, one that not only immediately appeals to the eye, but can also be lived with afterwards. Everything I have so far written herein on this subject comes within the scope of technique, and anyone who is prepared to give it adequate study and practice should be able to produce a satisfying picture.

But to create a picture that far transcends even the best snapshot requires more than this and might well be described as a flair or, if you like, a seeing eye that immediately

Plate 4 Great Gable from Lingmell Beck

appreciates the artistic merit of a particular mountain scene. And strangely enough those who possess this rare gift usually produce a certain type of picture which is indelibly stamped with their personality; so much so that it is often possible to name the photographer as soon as their work is displayed. And, moreover, while this especial artistic trait may be developed after long application of the basic principles of composition, the fact remains that it is not the camera that really matters, for it is merely a tool, but the person behind the viewfinder, who, when satisfied with the design of his or her subject, ultimately and quite happily releases the shutter.

To painters, composition is relatively easy, because they can make it conform to the basic principles of art by moving a tree to one side of the picture, or by completely removing a house from the foreground, or by inducing a stream to flow in another direction, or by accentuating the real subject, if it happens to be a mountain, by moving it or by increasing or decreasing its angles to suit their tastes. Photographers on the other hand have to move themselves and their camera here and there in order to get these objects in the right position in their viewfinder. When you move to one side to improve the position of one of them, another is thrown out of place, or perhaps the lighting is altered. In many cases, therefore, a compromise is the only solution, because if too much time is spent in solving this problem the mood may change, and the opportunity could be lost. It is just this element in mountain photography that brings it into line with sport, and, like golf, it can be both interesting and exasperating. Of course, critics can sit in a comfortable chair by a warm fire at home and pull a photograph to pieces. They probably do not realise that the person taking the picture may have been wandering about knee-deep in a slimy bog, or that a bitterly cold wind was sweeping across a lofty ridge and making his teeth chatter, or that the light was failing, or that he had crawled out on a rocky spur with a hundred-foot drop on either side to get the subject properly composed.

Assuming, therefore, both lighting and cloudscape are favourable, what are the essential features of good composition? In the first place, you must select a pleasing object that is accentuated by tonal contrast as the centre of interest; in the second you must place this object in the most attractive position in the frame or picture space; and in the third you must choose a strong and appropriate foreground. Or, in other words, when the weather is favourable the success or failure of your photograph will depend entirely upon the *viewpoint*.

Thus, if your subject happens to be Great Gable, I may be able to help you with a few hints about four of the illustrations in this book. It is generally agreed that the western aspect of this mountain is the finest and it looks its best on a sunny afternoon with high cloud overhead. But you must first decide whether you wish to take a picture of the majestic peak itself, or of its superb placing between the adjacent fells; the former depending upon the foregrounds available within close range, and the latter from a long distance.

Let us begin with the nearest possible coign of vantage as shown in Plate 4, where Lingmell Beck provides the foreground interest and where a vertical frame and wide-angle lens are essential. But owing to the proximity of the mountain emphasis is concentrated on the Napes Ridges only, while the elevation and nobility of the peak are not revealed. If we go further back to near Burnthwaite we obtain by the same technique a rather foreshortened picture of it, where the only useful foreground consists of the wall and tree on the right. By retreating still further to Wasdale Green we get a more comprehensive view and can use a normal 50 mm lens, but as will be seen in Plate 5 the foreground lacks interest. If, on the other hand, we go still further back to the side-road leading to Brackenclose and Wasdale Head Hall, and walk beside the stream to a point near the confluence of Mosedale and Lingmell Becks, we will discover a perfect foreground of tree and river together with a satisfactory view of our mountain at its correct elevation, as shown in

Plate 5 Great Gable from Wasdale Green

Plate 6 Great Gable from Lingmell Beck

Plate 7 Yewbarrow, Great Gable and Lingmell from Wastwater

Plate 6. An alternative viewpoint that reveals a similar elevation of the Gable, but with a different lead-in, is portrayed in Plate 37, and those who are prepared to ascend Lingmell will secure the most dynamic shot, as shown in Plate 36. Finally, if you wish to photograph Great Gable from a distant coign of vantage there is no more effective foreground than Wastwater, where from the foot of the lake the eye is drawn straight to it and reveals its central situation between Yewbarrow and Lingmell, as shown in Plate 7. Whenever you take a shot of any of the Lakeland Peaks, remember that it will be improved not only by placing a lake, a stream, a bridge, a figure or a group of walkers in the foreground, but also on occasion by introducing a tree or cottage or some object whose size if known will impart both interest and scale to your picture.

In conclusion, I would call your attention to the dramatic possibilities of photographing sunsets in colour; for by placing a still or slightly rippling lake in the foreground you will immensely enhance the whole picture by capturing the colour reflected by the water as well as that already appearing in the sky.

Notes
1 In case readers are interested in the photographic equipment used by my father, I can disclose that on the many occasions he was asked this question, his reply was, 'Since the availability of 35 mm film I have always used Leica cameras, replacing them as new models appeared.' In his last years he used an M2 with 35, 50 and 90 mm lenses for monochrome with Kodak Plus X film; for colour work he used a Leicaflex with 28, 50, 90 and 135 mm lenses, plus a 45/90 mm zoom, in conjunction with his favourite Kodachrome 25.
2 Some years before my father died he presented the collection of black and white negatives he had amassed over a period of more than half a century to the Royal Photographic Society and they now form part of their archive. They wish it to be known that prints from these can be supplied for an appropriate fee.

Photography in the different groups

I have often been asked 'What is the best view *of* such and such a mountain?' or 'What is the most striking view *from* so and so?' These are difficult questions, because the answers depend so much on one's tastes, which are influenced in no small degree by atmospheric conditions on any particular occasion. The present volume seems to be a convenient medium for an attempt to offer some guidance on this very debatable question, and while there are doubtless many who will disagree with my opinions, I shall give them for what they are worth. Where possible I have appended references to appropriate examples already portrayed in one or other of my works, as follows:

LL: *Lakeland Through the Lens*
LH: *Lakeland Holiday*
LJ: *Lakeland Journey*
OLF: *Over Lakeland Fells*
CC: *Climbing with a Camera*
LP: *The Lakeland Peaks* (the present work).

The number indicates the plate in the particular volume, to which I have added the most suitable time of day for photographing the subject (GMT). It should be noted that the examples given were not necessarily taken at the best time or season.

The suggestions are arranged according to the grouping system adopted throughout this work and under two headings: (1) The best pictorial views *of* the groups or their separate tops; (2) The most striking views *from* the groups. In both cases foreground interest is obviously of paramount importance since it bears a direct relationship to the pictorial rendering of the main subject.

The best pictorial views of the groups
The southern aspect of the Scafells
(*a*) From Border End. 11 a.m. or 4 p.m. LL 94; CC 68; LP 3.
(*b*) From Grey Friar to the north of the cairn. 11 a.m. or 3 p.m. OLF 4; LP 232; CC 62.
(*c*) From Harter Fell in Eskdale, on the western slopes to avoid Hard Knott, 11 a.m. or 3 p.m. LH 52; LP 23; CC 66.
(*d*) From Long Top on Crinkle Crags. 11 a.m. or 3 p.m. LJ 33; LP 216; CC 54.

Scafell Pike from Upper Eskdale. 11 a.m. or 3 p.m. LH 1; CC 99.

Scafell from Lingmell. 7 p.m. onwards, May or June. LL 47 & 86; LP 13 & 29.

Great End from the western slopes of Glaramara. 9 a.m., May or June.

Lingmell from The Corridor. 11 a.m., April, May or June. LP 17 & 18.

Great Gable
(*a*) From Wasdale, 6 p.m., May or June. LL 76; LH 50; OLF 35; LP 37; CC 72.
(*b*) From Lingmell. 6 p.m., May or June. OLF 32; LP 36; CC 106.
(*c*) From Haystacks. 7 p.m., June. LH 38; LP 102

Pillar from Green Gable. 11 a.m., May or June. LL 60; LP 88.

Yewbarrow from Netherbeck. 4 p.m. onwards, May or June. LL 65; LH 48; LP 89.

High Stile
(*a*) From Lanthwaite Hill, 6 p.m., May or June, OLF 61; LP 91.
(*b*) From Dale Head. 11 a.m., May or June.
(*c*) From Robinson. 11 a.m., May or June. OLF 79.

Dale Head from Loweswater Village, any time of day.

Skiddaw
(*a*) From Lodore. 6 p.m., Spring to Autumn.
(*b*) From Castle Head. 6 p.m., May or June. OLF 85; LP 132.

Blencathra
(*a*) From Clough Head. 10 a.m. or 4 p.m.
(*b*) From the east. 11 a.m. LP 137.
(*c*) From St John's in the Vale. CC 22.

Helvellyn
(*a*) From Birkhouse Moor. 11 a.m. OLF 87; CC 17.
(*b*) From Striding Edge. 11 a.m. LL 16; OLF 88; LP 147; CC 18.
(*c*) From St Sunday Crag. 11 a.m.

Fairfield from High Street. 11 a.m. LP 167.

High Street from Kidsty Pike. 11 a.m. LP 176.

High Street from Harter Fell. CC 16; noon LP 182.

Harter Fell in Mardale from Haweswater. 10 a.m. LL 12; OLF 106; LP 177; CC 15.

The Langdale Pikes
(*a*) From Elterwater. 11 a.m. or sunset. LL 95; CC 47.
(*b*) From Chapel Stile. 3 p.m. onwards, Spring or Autumn. LL 96; LP 186; CC 55.

Bowfell
(*a*) From Eskdale, 11 a.m. or 4 p.m. LL 89; LH 59; LP 207.
(*b*) From Long Top, Crinkle Crags. 11 a.m. or 4 p.m. LJ 36; LL 113; LP 203; CC 58.

Crinkle Crags
(*a*) From Red Tarn. 11 a.m. LJ 27 & 28.
(*b*) From Langdale. 9 a.m. LJ 26; CC 53.
(*c*) Long Top Buttress. 3 p.m. LJ 30.

Coniston Old Man from Coniston Water. 11 a.m. CC 55; from Torver. LP 219.

Dow Crag from Goat's Water. 11 a.m. LL 118; LP 225.

Wetherlam from Tarn Hows. 11 a.m. LJ 8; LP 239.

Harter Fell in Eskdale from above the Woolpack Inn. 4 p.m. LH 55; LP 247; CC 65.

Harter Fell in Eskdale from Dunnerdale. 11 a.m. CC 73; LP 250.

The most striking views from the groups
Scafell Pike. Great Gable and Sty Head. 11 a.m. or 4 p.m. LP 48.

Scafell
(*a*) Grasmoor Hills and the Gable. 4 p.m. LH 65; CC 105.
(*b*) Mosedale from Deep Ghyll. 4 p.m. LP 27; CC 104.
(*c*) Gable and the Pinnacle from Deep Ghyll. 4 p.m. LP 28.
(*d*) South from the summit cairn. 6 p.m. onwards. LH 70.

Great End
(*a*) Borrowdale and Skiddaw. 11 a.m. or 3 p.m. LL 41.
(*b*) The Gable and Sty Head from the northern slopes. 4 p.m. LJ 76; LP 47; CC 97.

Lingmell
(*a*) The Gable. 4 p.m. onwards. OLF 32; LP 36; CC 106.
(*b*) Sty Head. 4 p.m. onwards. OLF 31; LL 1 & 2.

(c) Mickledore and Hollow Stones. 6 p.m. onwards, May or June. OLF 34; LP 10.

(d) Scafell. 7 p.m. onwards, May or June. LL 47 & 86; LP 29; CC 104.

Great Gable

(a) Wastwater from the Sphinx Rock. 11 a.m. LL 80; LP 53; CC 10.

(b) The Grasmoor Hills. 11 a.m. or 3 p.m. LP 54.

Kirk Fell

(a) The Scafells. 6 p.m. CC 82; LP 57.

(b) The Gable. 3 p.m. CC 81; LP 58.

Glaramara

(a) Borrowdale. 11 a.m. or 3 p.m. CC 30.

(b) The Gable. 11 a.m. LJ 72; CC 30; LP 68.

(c) The Langdale Pikes. 5 p.m. LJ 73.

Pillar

(a) West face of the Pillar Rock. 4 p.m. onwards. LL 71; LP 78; CC 80.

(b) East face of the Pillar Rock. 11 a.m. LL 70; LP 74; CC 78.

(c) The Central Fells from just below the Great Doup. 5 p.m. onwards.

Yewbarrow. The Scafells from the Great Door. 6 p.m. onwards. LL 65; LP 90.

High Stile. The Central Fells. 6 p.m. OLF 52; LP 99; CC 40.

Fleetwith Pike. The Buttermere Valley. 11 a.m. CC 37.

Dale Head
(a) Newlands and Skiddaw. 4 p.m. onwards. OLF 78; CC 43.
(b) Honister, High Stile and Buttermere. 11 a.m. LP 109; CC 44.

Grasmoor. The Central Fells. 6 p.m. onwards. OLF 65; LP 131; CC 46.

Skiddaw
(a) Derwentwater from Latrigg. 10 a.m. LJ 49 & 50.
(b) Derwentwater from Carl Side. 10 a.m.
(c) The Grasmoor Hills. 11 a.m. LJ 46.

Blencathra. Looking across the lateral spurs to Derwentwater. 11 a.m. LL 21; LP 141; CC 21, and CC 24 at 4 p.m.

Helvellyn
(a) Striding Edge from the Abyss. 11 a.m. OLF 91; LL 17; LP 148; CC 19.
(b) The western Panorma. Up to midday. OLF 90; LP 152.

Fairfield
(a) Ullswater from St Sunday Crag. 6 p.m. OLF 101; LP 158; CC 20.
(b) Windermere from Nab Scar. 11 a.m. or 4 p.m.

High Street
(a) The western Panorama. 11 a.m. LP 167 & 168.
(b) Windermere from Thornthwaite Beacon. 11 a.m. or 4 p.m. LL 13.

Harter Fell in Mardale. Haweswater. 11 a.m. or 4 p.m. CC 16; LP 181.

The Langdale Pikes
(*a*) Harrison Stickle from Pike o'Stickle. 3 p.m. LL 106; LP 193;
    CC 52.
(*b*) Gimmer Crag from Pike o'Stickle. 4 p.m. LL 107 & 108;
    LP 192; CC 51.
(*c*) Pavey Ark from Stickle Tarn up to 2 p.m. CC 52; LP 189.

Bowfell. The Scafells. 11 a.m.

Crinkle Crags
(*a*) The Scafells. 11 a.m. LJ 33; LP 22 & 30; CC 54.
(*b*) Pike o'Blisco from Mickle Door up to noon. LJ 32; CC 57.

Pike o'Blisco. Great Langdale. 11 a.m. LJ 25.

Conniston Old Man. North-west to the Central Fells. 3 p.m.
LP 222.

Grey Friar. The Scafells. 2 p.m. OLF 4; LP 232, CC 62.

Wetherlam The Langdale Pikes from below Birk Fell. 11 a.m. or
3 p.m. LJ 20; LP 238.

Harter Fell in Eskdale. The Scafells and Upper Eskdale. 11 a.m.
or 3 p.m. LH 52; LP 23; CC 66.

Border End in Eskdale. The Lakeland Giants. 4 p.m. LL 94; CC 68;
CC frontispiece in colour; LP 3.

Notes on the Routes

The Lakeland Peaks are divided into *fourteen Mountain Groups* for the sake of convenience and easy reference. They commence with the Scafells, because Scafell Pike is the highest mountain in England and its ascent the most popular. The groups then follow each other in clockwise sequence throughout the district and end with the Coniston Group and Harter Fell in Eskdale. *The Routes* to the reigning peak in each group are also arranged clockwise so that they fit into the general scheme and thus avoid undue cross reference. *Descents* have been purposely omitted because when the ascents are reversed they obviously answer this requirement. These arrangements facilitate the choice of those routes which connect up with one another to form a *Traverse* of two, or even three, groups in one expedition, but their length will naturally depend upon the powers of the walker. *The Panorama* from the reigning peak in each group is always described at the end of its first ascent. Many of the routes involve the traverse of subsidiary tops and the conspicuous features revealed from them are noted in passing, in spite of the fact that there may be a similarity in the views if the peaks are adjacent.

Mountain navigation

The skills required to navigate safely and accurately are won only after long apprenticeship. As with many aspects of the mountaineer's craft, you would be well advised to seek expert instruction in techniques by going on a course or by going out with experienced friends.

The basic tools required are a map and compass. The map is the single most important, for without it a compass is worth little. Time should be spent studying the map and learning how mountain features are interpreted by the map makers. Contour lines are the most complex to understand for they show the shape and form of the hills and their steepness and height above sea level. Learning to read contour lines will help you to create an image in your mind's eye of what the mountains will look like. Once out in the field, apply your interpretation to what you actually see and discover whether or not the two match up.

When using the map to identify features, you should try to work with it set so that if the map was true to life size you could lay it over the ground and all features would match both on the ground and on the map. This is called *orientating the map*. Inevitably this will entail reading the map upside down or even from the side but it will make it considerably easier to understand.

You must also familiarise yourself with the various ways in which roads and footpaths, lakes and rivers, and all manner of other things are shown. There are two scales of map that are of interest to the walker. One is the 2 cm to 1 km scale OS Landranger series (1:50 000) and the other the 4 cm to 1 km OS Outdoor Leisure series (1:25 000). The latter scale, being some-what larger, affords the mountain navigator much more detail both in contour and crag features and also by showing walls and fences.

The compass is an integral part of the toolkit and the most commonly used, by far, is the Silva type 4. For the compass to be of any use it should have a long base plate with a metric measuring scale and a device called a roamer which splits grid squares on the map into tenths enabling the user to work out grid references accurately. The magnetic needle of the compass is contained in the compass housing – a circular housing marked off in degrees from 0 to 360 and correspondingly marked N, S, E and W. The compass housing must also have a set of parallel lines underneath, which are called orientating lines. A small magnifying glass incorporated into the base plate is a useful extra tool for identifying vague features on the map.

In order to take a bearing from one point to another you must follow some basic steps. 1. Line up an edge of the compass along the intended direction of travel. The compass housing should be at the starting end of the journey with the direction of travel arrow pointing to where you want to go. 2. Hold the compass firmly in place and turn the compass housing until the red orientating lines on the base of the housing are parallel with the grid lines that run vertically up the map, (the Eastings). There is an arrow joining the middle two lines and this should point to the top of the map. 3. Take the compass off the map and add on the magnetic variation. In the Lake District in 1996 it was 5 degrees, and it decreases by about 0.5 degrees every four years. 4. Hold the compass in front of you and turn until you line the red part of the magnetic compass needle up with the North mark on the compass housing rim. The direction to walk in is the one where the direction of travel arrow points.

This is a very basic explanation of the technique and if you are unsure of how to operate it you must seek expert advice before you can expect to rely on it in a life or death situation.

It is not enough simply to be capable of performing the previously mentioned tasks. Successful navigation relies on what can best be described as 'mountain sense'. This is a feeling and an awareness for the things that are around you combined with sensible and logical thought processes and close attention to detail.

You will also need to know how to measure distances along the ground. This is most accurately done by pace counting. An average person will take about 60–65 double paces to 100 metres over easy walking ground. The rougher it is the more you might take. The skill of pacing can only be learned through a great deal of practice but it can become a reliable aid to successful navigation. Pacing and timing go together though the latter, due to countless stops to check map and compass, can be difficult to use accurately and is at best a rough guide.

To work out how long it will take to cover a certain distance you must consider both the length of the journey and the height gained. If no height is gained you would normally only consider the distance. However, if the going is rough it may occasionally take more time to descend than it would to ascend.

As a foundation from which to work, take an average walking pace of 1 kilometre every 12 minutes (1.2 minutes per 100 metres) and add 1.5 minutes for every 10 metre contour line crossed in ascent. Thus, if you have a section of your journey to cover that is 1500 metres long and goes from the 200 metre contour to the 360 metre contour, you have:

Distance $15 \times 1.2 = 18$ minutes, plus

Height gain $16 \times 1.5 = 24$ minutes

Total time for the section = 42 minutes

In terms of measuring the distance whilst walking one would multiply one's own average number of paces per 100 metres by 15. It is always better to count in units of 100 metres because it is difficult to keep track of the running total when a large figure is involved. Pebbles or a special click counter are useful aids to remembering how far you have gone.

If you become lost or disorientated, which you inevitably will sometime, try not to become too flustered. There are some important basics to staying safe. Do not follow streams or ravines over steep ground and try to avoid having to find your way down ground interspersed with crags and cliffs. Open grass slopes are much safer.

Mountain rescue

If you or your companion sustains an injury that is incapacitating seek shelter at the earliest opportunity. Here your emergency clothing, survival bag and spare food will come in useful. Try to identify your position on the map and mark it down. You could accost passing fellow walkers to fetch help but if you need to leave anyone behind to go for help yourself make sure you know where the rescue team can find them. Go to a telephone box and dial 999 and ask for Mountain Rescue. If you decide that it is foolish to move, you can try to attract attention by using the International Distress signal which is six long flashes or whistle blasts followed by a minute's pause and then repeated. The reply is similar but flashes or blasts are only three.

Brocken spectres

These phenomena are confined to hill country, and in consequence may, with luck, be observed by walkers on the Lakeland Peaks, especially if they are on a ridge enclosing a combe filled with mist. They appear to be gigantic shadows seen on the mist and were first viewed on the Brocken in Germany, hence the name, but are said to be an optical illusion because the shadow is quite close and of actual size. It is usually only possible for each walker to see his own spectre.

Glories

These appear, in similar circumstances, as a coloured ring round the shadow cast by the walker on the mist. Each member of a walking party can only see his or her own 'glory'.

The Scafell Group

Scafell Pike	978 metres	3209 feet
Scafell	964metres	3163 feet
Ill Crag	935 metres	3068 feet
Broad Crag	934 metres	3064 feet
Great End	910 metres	2985 feet
Lingmell	807 metres	2648 feet
Slight Side	762 metres	2500 feet
Esk Hause	*759 metres*	*2490 feet*
Sty Head	*488 metres*	*1600 feet*

OS Map: Landranger 89 West Cumbria
    Outdoor Leisure 6 South Western Area

The approach to Wasdale

The importance of Wasdale as a Lakeland climbing centre has been well known throughout the years and is due to the proximity of Scafell, Scafell Pike, Great Gable and Pillar. All these groups of hills display some of the finest subjects for both artist and photographer, and in my early days we all had to accept the lack of amenities at the hotel, just to be there on the spot. But today I am glad to say that the improvement in accomodation and food is immense and on my last visit I was delighted not only with them but also with the excellence of the service.

However, to reach the hotel most visitors come by car and when the foot of the lake is revealed ahead they must be greatly impressed by the magnificence of The Screes, a strange feature that is unique in our British hills. I felt therefore that the inclusion of just one photograph of them in this book would be welcomed by readers, although the gully climbs and the charming walks over Illgill Head and Whin Rigg are omitted from this work.

Plate 8 The Wastwater Screes

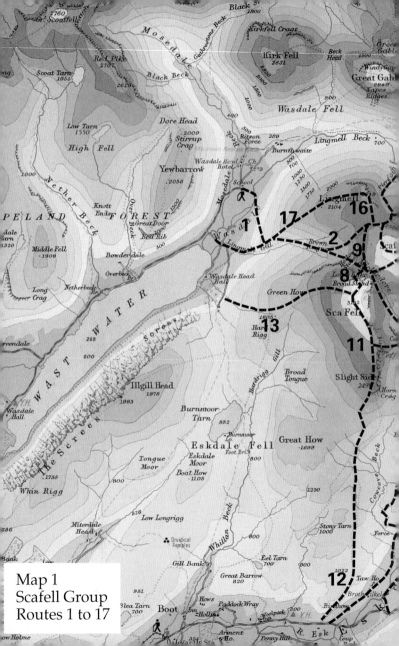

Map 1
Scafell Group
Routes 1 to 17

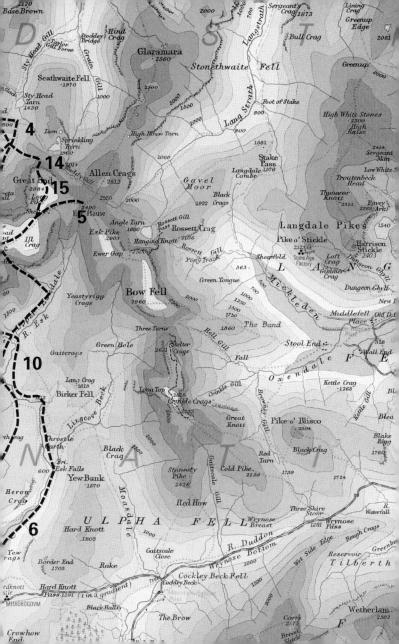

Scafell Pike

Route 1. Wasdale, Brown Tongue and Mickledore. Leave Wasdale Head by the Gosforth road, and after passing the old school, GR 186084, turn L for the path across the field. Cross the bridge over Lingmell Beck, and turn R, south, for the path which rises gently round the flank of Lingmell with increasingly extensive vistas along Wastwater to The Screes. When Lingmell Gill comes into view ahead (after crossing the path rising to Lingmell), traverse L above it, to reach the path rising from Brackenclose. Ascend the path and cross the stream at the foot of Brown Tongue. A well-marked path ascends this steep spur on its south side, i.e. not on the crest of the tongue, with Pikes Crag looming on the horizon. When the gradient eases off, Hollow Stones will be perceived ahead stretching across the great basin below Pikes Crag. Take the path rising ahead, well below the precipices of Scafell Crag. Do not ascend the scree shoot on R, but go straight ahead, past a conspicuous large boulder, up the scree to the col of Mickledore. From the narrow crest of Mickledore, take the path L, north-east, which leads over the boulder-strewn slopes to the great cairn on the summit of Scafell Pike.

The panorama is extensive with uninterrupted views in all directions. On a clear day all the engirdling hills can be seen and the distant prospect comprises Skiddaw and Blencathra to the north; the great Helvellyn range on the eastern horizon and the Coniston Fells and Harter Fell to the south. Among the more prominent of the nearer hills Pillar dominates the north-western view, and Great Gable to the north rises from the confines of Sty Head, with a glimpse of Derwentwater above the tarn. Bowfell appears less interesting, to the south-east and Windermere to its R. Scafell appears to the south-west. The western vista is striking with the sea glittering into the dim distance where the Isle of Man may be perceived in clear weather. The 'Eskdale Cairn' or 'south peak', about 150 m south of the summit, is worth visiting because it reveals an amazing bird's-eye view of the upper Eskdale valley with the river over 600 m (2000 ft) below.

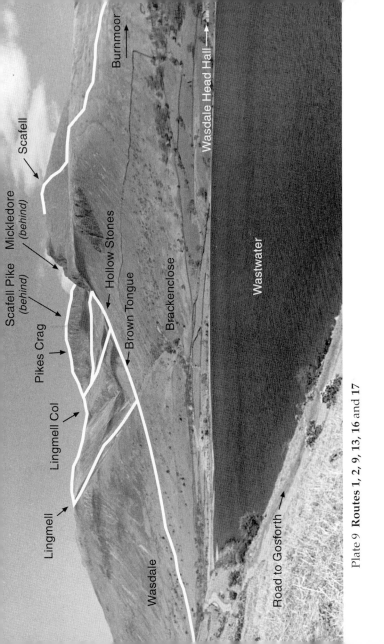

Plate 9 **Routes 1, 2, 9, 13, 16 and 17**

Plate 10 **Routes 1 and 2** to the main Scafell Crags

Plate 11 **Route 1**—Scafell Pike from Scafell

Plate 12 **Route 1**—Fell walkers resting by the cairn on Scafell Pike

Route 2. Wasdale, Brown Tongue and Lingmell Col. This is a less arduous ascent than Route 1, but it follows the same course as far as the top of Brown Tongue. At GR 201073 bear to the L and follow the cairns and path which rise gently to Lingmell Col, to the north of Pikes Crag. From the col, a cairned path ascends the rough slopes on R, and winds about over the easiest gradients and joins Route 1 again just below the cairn on the reigning peak.

Route 3. Sty Head and Piers Gill. Reach Sty Head either from Seathwaite via Stockley Bridge or from Wasdale Head by the path across the south flank of Great Gable. From the Mountain Rescue stretcher box at GR 219095, take the path south-east to Skew Gill. On reaching the mouth of this conspicuous ravine, take the lower path, indistinct but with cairns, which traverses the fellside south-westwards. There is a short rocky scramble where the route crosses Grainy Gills (two streams unnamed on the OS 1:25 000 map, north of Stand Crag). From below Stand Crag, with a prospect of Piers Gill straight ahead below Lingmell, descend the steep ground west to cross Greta Gill well below its ravine. Now join the path L of Piers Gill, above the confluence of Piers Gill and Greta Gill. The path generally follows a line fairly close to the ravine, although there is a short scramble at a rockband away from the gill, north of Middleboot Knotts. At GR 214079, the well-marked Corridor Route (Route 4) comes in from the L, and after crossing the stream ascend westwards for Lingmell Col. Now follow Route 2 on the L to the summit of Scafell Pike.

Note – Walkers coming from Wasdale Head need not ascend the well-trodden stony path to Sty Head, since they may reach Skew Gill by using the path near Lingmell Beck and the old zigzag path east, near Spouthead Gill. From here a short ascent east leads to Skew Gill. Alternatively from Wasdale Head, walkers may use the path near Lingmell Beck then ascend southwards on the path alongside the full length of Piers Gill.

Plate 13 The final section of **Route 2**

Plate 14 **Route 2**—The north-western prospect from the summit

Plate 15 Sty Head—morning mists clearing from the Scafell Pikes

Great End →

Corridor Route

Skew Gill

To Piers Gill

Sty Head

Wasdale Track

Plate 16 **Routes 3, 4** and **14** are well seen from just below Sty Head

Route 4. Sty Head and the Corridor Route. Follow Route 3 to Skew Gill, but take the steeper path out of it. The path rises sharply at first until the more gentle sections of the Corridor Route are attained. Follow the path to the junction above Piers Gill and then keep to Route 3 to the summit of Scafell Pike. Those wishing to take a short cut from the top of Piers Gill, or from the point (GR 216079) east of the head of Piers Gill, will ascend the defile between Broad Crag and Scafell Pike and then join Route 5 to the summit of the latter. The views to the north from the Corridor Route are especially fine of Great Gable, where the maze of tracks leading to its summit may easily be perceived. There are also bird's-eye views into Piers Gill on the R, together with a magnificent frontal view of the crags of Lingmell.

Route 5. Esk Hause, Ill Crag and Broad Crag. This is one of the most clearly marked and well-cairned paths in Lakeland. It leaves west from Esk Hause and rises gently via Calf Cove to the hause on the horizon with Great End on R. Just short of this hause there is a spring, the last place where a drink may be obtained on this route. The path goes up and down over a perfect maze of rough boulders, on to the plateau of Ill Crag. A short detour south may be made to the summit of Ill Crag. The path for Scafell Pike falls to a col before traversing the plateau of Broad Crag. A short, very rough scramble may be made to Broad Crag summit. The path for the Pike drops sharply to the col at the head of Little Narrowcove, and then sweeps round to the large cairn perched on the roof of England.

Plate 17 **Route 4** crosses Piers Gill, at its exit on the R, immediately below the summit crags of Lingmell

Plate 18 **Route 3**—Lingmell and Piers Gill

Plate 19 Retrospect from **Route 5** near Esk Hause. **Route 31** to Allen Crags

Route 6. Brotherilkeld, Esk Falls and Little Narrowcove. Walk to the L of Brotherilkeld farmyard, near the foot of Hardknott Pass, and pick up the path well above the River Esk on L. Yew Crags tower above on R, and after passing below them drop down gradually to join the bank of the river. This sweeps round to the L as far as Lingcove Bridge, the packhorse bridge over Lingcove Beck. Cross the bridge, and ascend the grassy banks on R of Esk Falls. These falls are at GR 226037; there is a series of falls upstream from here. Pass through the gap between Green Crag and Throstlehow Crag, and turn sharp L at the bend of the river. Follow this with Scafell rising ahead and then when Scafell Pike is revealed to the north, keep to the right of the river until about opposite Cam Spout. Now make for Dow Crag (known to climbers as Esk Buttress) and cross the river at any convenient spot. Pass below the precipices of this fine escarpment, and then Little Narrowcove will be disclosed beyond it. Ascend beside the beck, with a magnificent surround of Chambers Crag, Green Crag and Ill Crag, until the col at the head of Little Narrowcove is attained. Turn to L and follow Route 5 to Scafell Pike summit.

The views of the upper Esk valley unfolded from Great Moss are some of the most profound in Lakeland. The great ridge is crowned by the giants of the district and forms a stupendous horseshoe from Slight Side in the west to Long Top (Crinkle Crags) in the east, and includes Scafell, Scafell Pike, Ill Crag, Esk Pike and Bowfell.

Route 7. Taw House, Cam Spout and Mickledore. Taw House may be reached by a farm road from the valley road in Eskdale or from Brotherilkeld by a footbridge over the River Esk. Follow the path to Scale Bridge, at Scale Gill. Thence bear L and ascend the grassy zigzag path to the open fell, where Slight Side is revealed ahead, and continue to the stream of Damas Dubs at GR 214033. Continue along the path north-north-eastwards then north, to the shoulder of fell at GR 221044, east of High Scarth

Green Crag

Ill Crag

Throstlehov Crag

To Upper Esk Valley

Track to brid over Lingcov Beck

Esk Falls

Plate 20 **Route 6**—Esk Falls

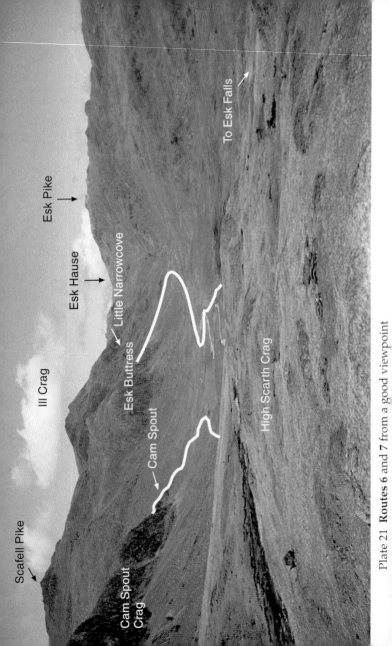

Plate 21 **Routes 6** and **7** from a good viewpoint

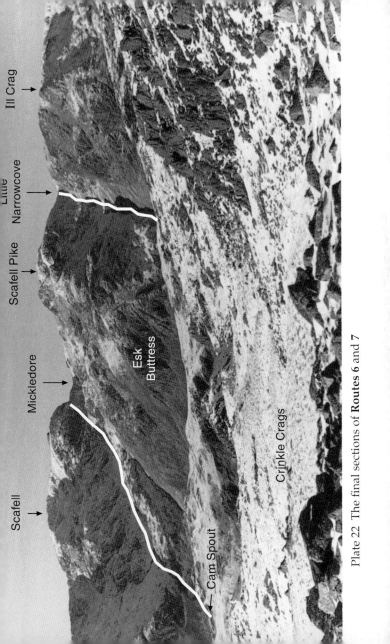

Plate 22 The final sections of **Routes 6 and 7**

Crag. The whole of upper Eskdale is disclosed ahead. Down below on L a sheepfold will be seen; descend slightly to this. Follow the path, east past Sampson's Stones, below the shattered cliffs of Cam Spout Crag, and swing round to L. Cross the stream emerging from Cam Spout and ascend the path R of this rocky gorge. The path keeps close to the stream, and Mickledore will soon be seen on the horizon. Make for it, ascend the loose scree, and join Route 1 on the narrow crest.

Scafell

Route 8. Wasdale, Brown Tongue and Lord's Rake. Follow Route 1 from Wasdale Head to Hollow Stones. On approaching Mickledore ascend the scree shoot on R, which leads to the foot of Lord's Rake, below Scafell Crag. Lord's Rake is the narrow ravine on R at the top of the scree. Scramble up the steep, loose scree gully to a narrow col. From just short of this col, on the L, take the path on to a shelf which rises sensationally above the lower reaches of Deep Ghyll (Deep Gill), and is known as the West Wall Traverse. This leads into the gloomy recesses of Deep Ghyll itself where Scafell Pinnacle rises on L and Deep Ghyll Buttress on R. The rift is characterised by loose scree and great care is necessary in ascending it to the open fell at the top of the ghyll. A detour can be made round the rim of the chasm to L, and with care a short scramble can be made on to the pinnacle of Pisgah. This detour unfolds one of Lakeland's most impressive landscapes, including Deep Ghyll Buttress, whose top may also be reached from the head of Deep Ghyll. Walk across the stony ground and saddle south-west to the summit cairn of Scafell, for the view to the south. This comprises all the southern hills, in which Harter Fell is prominent, the sands of the Duddon beyond, and Morecambe Bay in the far distance.

From the col on Lord's Rake an alternative is to continue in the straight line followed thus far via another small col and a stony hollow, to the exit to Lord's Rake on the open fell. Here turn to L and ascend the stony slope to Scafell summit.

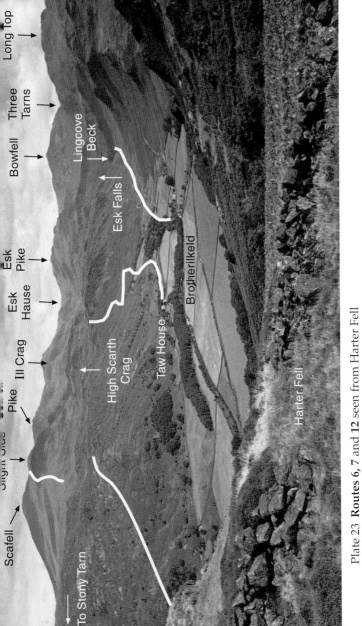

Plate 23 **Routes 6, 7** and **12** seen from Harter Fell

Note 1 – There is a path between the foot of Lord's Rake and Mickledore. Thus Lord's Rake provides a linking route between Scafell and Scafell Pike. Foxes Tarn provides an alternative way between these two mountains: from the saddle north-east of Scafell summit cairn, take the path south-east down to the tarn, then turn L to descend the gully with stream, to join Route 7 coming up from Cam Spout for Mickledore.

Note 2 – Broad Stand at the edge of Mickledore gives the shortest way on to Scafell from Mickledore, but it is a rock climbing route only, and *not* for fellwalkers. Equally, Rake's Progress is a rock climbing route only, making a link between Mickledore and the foot of Lord's Rake.

Route 9. Sty Head, the Corridor Route and Hollow Stones. From Sty Head follow the Corridor Route, Route 4, to Lingmell Col. Traverse the slopes south-west, descending slightly, then follow the path south, below the precipices of Pikes Crag and Pulpit Rock on L. Scafell rises ahead, and this route reveals one of the best prospects of its savage precipices. Join Route 8 at the scree shoot leading to Lord's Rake.

Route 10. Brotherilkeld, Esk Falls, Cam Spout and Mickle-dore. Follow Route 6 as far as the River Esk at Great Moss. Cross the river at any convenient place and head for the path on R of the rocky gorge of Cam Spout. Ascend the path close to the stream north-westwards and then the loose scree to Mickle-dore. Follow the path below the Scafell bastions to the foot of Lord's Rake. Then follow Route 8 for the summit.

Note – Before reaching Mickledore on the above route, there is an alternative way to Scafell summit, via Foxes Tarn. To follow this alternative, look for a stony gully with stream rising to the L, close to but below the base of the magnificent East Buttress of Scafell Crag. The gully leads directly to the tarn, from which a path leads R, north-west, to the saddle north-east of Scafell summit.

Plate 24 **Route 8** can only be photographed late on a summer evening

Scafell

Scafell Pinnacle

Pisgah

Deep Ghyll

West Wall Traverse

Lords Rake

To Wasdale

Rakes Progress

Hollow Stones

Mickledore

West Wall Traverse

Lords Rake

Broad Stand

Mickledore

Plate 25 The hardest and final section of **Route 8** to Scafell

Plate 26 The exit of **Route 8**

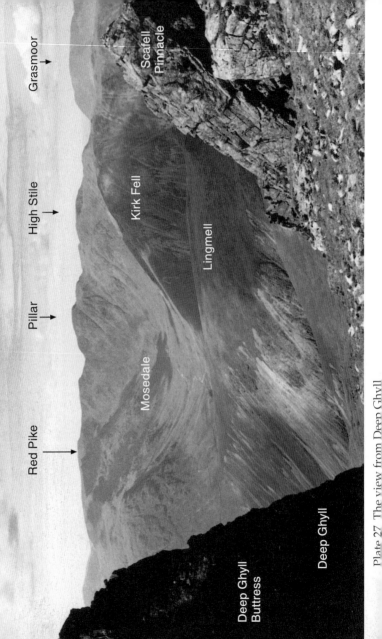

Plate 27 The view from Deep Ghyll

Plate 28 Looking back on the exit of Deep Ghyll

Pulpit Rock

Pikes Crag

Mickledore

Scafell

Deep Ghyll

Lords Rake

Route 11. Taw House and Cam Spout Crag. Follow Route 7 as far as the path at How Beck above Cam Spout. Cross the stream here and make for the edge of Cam Spout Crag, crossing the boulder-strewn slopes to the south. Keep near the edge of the precipices, with impressive views of upper Eskdale far below. As the ridge narrows, bear to R and then follow its crest until the ridge of Long Green is attained. Turn to R and keep to the ridge path which eventually leads to the cairn on Scafell.

Route 12. Wha House and Slight Side. Start at the Eskdale road at GR 201009 near Wha House Farm. Cross the stile and walk up the path north-east. Pass through a sheepfold and then follow the path, known as the Terrace Route, beside a wall. This section of the route unfolds some fine views of Hard Knott and Bowfell. Follow the path north, across Catcove Beck, and forge ahead towards Slight Side, keeping well above Cowcove Beck on R. Ascend the steep path to the rocky top of Slight Side, and follow the ridge path via Long Green which leads to the cairn on Scafell.

A longer approach from Eskdale starts at the Woolpack Inn. Leave the inn by the gate at the back and walk up the path until it emerges on the shore of Eel Tarn. Pass round the far side of this sheet of water, and then ascend the fell gently in a north-easterly direction. Follow a path past a sheepfold north of Stony Tarn, before ascending to the wide hause south-west of Cat Cove. Now cross the fellside north-north-east, to join the path from Wha House south of Slight Side.

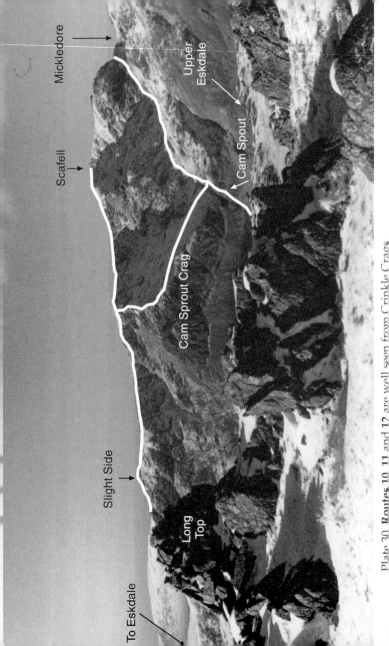

Plate 30. **Routes 10, 11 and 12 are well seen from Crinkle Crags.**

Mickledore

Scafell

Slight Side

Cam Spout

Upper Eskdale

Cam Spout Crag

Long Top

To Eskdale

Route 13. Burnmoor direct. A well-marked path runs from Wasdale to Boot, and also, from near Burnmoor Tarn, to the Woolpack Inn, Eskdale. From the summit of the pass, north of the tarn, you can make your own route north-east to Green How and then to the summit of Scafell which rises ahead to the east.

Note – From the path on the Wasdale side of the pass, at the footbridge across Hollow Gill and Groove Gill, another variation is possible. Ascend the tongue south-east, to pick up a thin path between the gills. This continues eastwards as a thin cairned path on to Green How and further, over the steep stony slopes, to the depression immediately north of Scafell summit.

Great End

Route 14. Sty Head and Skew Gill. From the Mountain Rescue stretcher box, GR 219095, at Sty Head, follow the path south-east, downhill at first, to Skew Gill and walk up the lower reaches of this impressive ravine. It bends round to L near the top and the exit provides a pleasant scramble. Continue ahead to a small col, with The Band on L. Now ascend the ridge southwards. Scramble up a short scree gully, then steep rocks lead to the cairns on the summit of Great End. Note the head of Cust's Gully on L; the gully is identified by a chockstone forming an arch. Before crossing the vast summit plateau, note also the superb retrospect of Great Gable and Sty Head Tarn, with Grasmoor R of the peak.

Route 15. Esk Hause direct. Take the path west from Esk Hause and bear to R, north-west, after about 250 m. The ascent is over rough boulders and the best views are obtained by keeping close to the edge of the precipices as the summit is approached. The cairns stand back on the L, but they do not reveal the finest prospects.

The panorama to the north is one of the most magnificent in

Lakeland and is observed to the best advantage from the south exit of Central Gully which splits the vast precipices on the northern aspect of the mountain where they drop away sensationally in the foreground. The dark waters of Sprinkling Tarn appear over 300 m (1000 ft) below and the eye follows the dim recesses of Grains Gill and, after passing over the green strath of Borrowdale, skims the surface of Derwentwater to rest finally upon the noble form of Skiddaw on the distant horizon. Blencathra will be seen to rise majestically on R of this mountain.

An easier route is to follow Route 5 to the hause west of Calf Cove, and to then bear R through the boulders for the two summit cairns.

Lingmell

Route 16. From Lingmell Col. Follow Routes 2, 3, 4 or 9 as far as the col and then bear to the north-west, ascending by the edge of the precipices on the right. The view to the north over Sty Head is magnificent, but the most spectacular prospect is of Great Gable, which is best seen by descending slightly beyond the cairn.

Route 17. From Brackenclose direct. From the car-park at GR 182075, walk past Brackenclose and cross Lingmell Gill by a footbridge. Keep to the grassy spur of Lingmell all the way, north-east, crossing a stone wall at height about 325 m. From the top of this spur a broad grassy ridge extends right up to the summit of Lingmell and reveals striking views of Wasdale, Mosedale and Pillar on L, together with a remarkable prospect of Hollow Stones and Scafell on R.

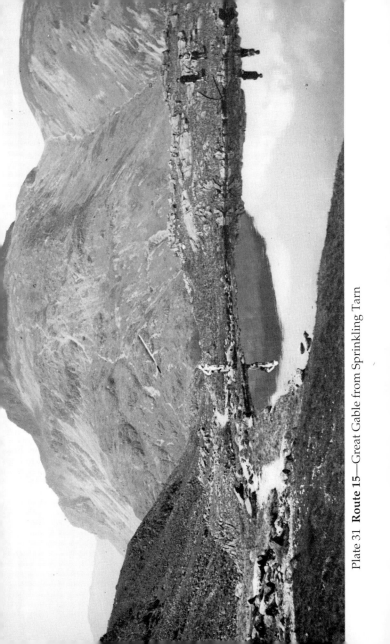

Plate 31 **Route 15**—Great Gable from Sprinkling Tarn

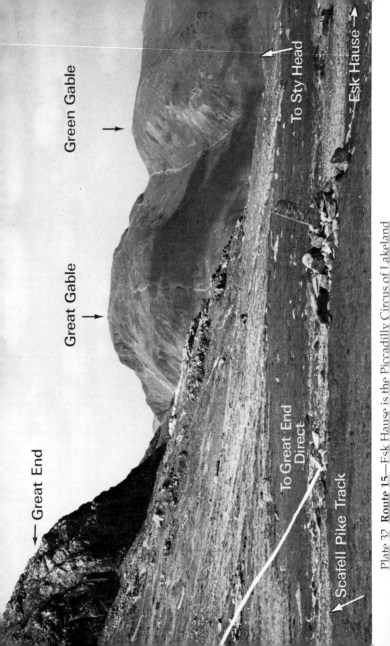

Plate 32 **Route 15**—Esk Hause is the Piccadilly Circus of Lakeland

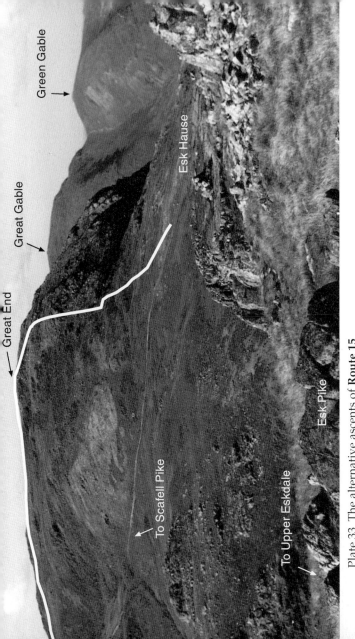

Plate 33 The alternative ascents of **Route 15**

Plate 21, Band 15. Scintillite. Type from the north mit of Central Sichuan Gun Field, from ...

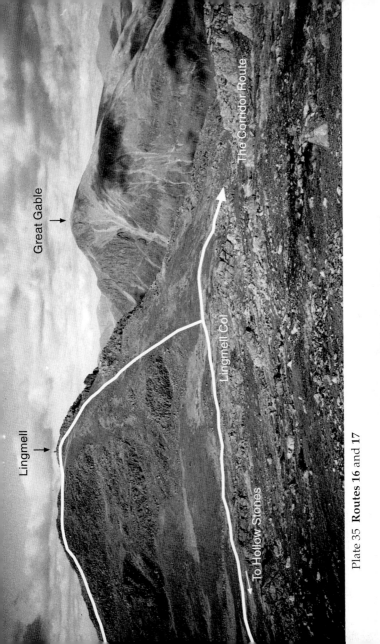

Great Gable

Lingmell

Lingmell Col

The Corridor Route

To Hollow Stones

Plate 35 **Routes 16 and 17**

Plate 36 Great Gable from Lingmell, a good viewpoint

The Gable group

Great Gable	899 metres	2949 feet
Kirk Fell	802 metres	2631 feet
Green Gable	801 metres	2628 feet
Allen Crags	785 metres	2575 feet
Glaramara	783 metres	2569 feet
Brandreth	715 metres	2346 feet
Grey Knotts	697 metres	2287 feet
Base Brown	646 metres	2119 feet
Bessyboot	c551 metres	1807 feet
Honister Hause	*363 metres*	*1190 feet*

OS Map: Landranger 89 West Cumbria
　　　　　Outdoor Leisure 4 North Western Area
　　　　　Outdoor Leisure 6 South Western Area

Great Gable
Route 18. Wasdale, Gavel Neese and the Sphinx Ridge. Leave the car-park at Wasdale Head by the lane which passes the church and leads to the farmstead of Burnthwaite. Take the Sty Head track, and after crossing the footbridge over Gable Beck coming down from Beck Head, bear to L up the path which keeps to the crest of Gavel Neese. The ascent of this grassy spur is steep and arduous and it ultimately gives place to slippery scree, where the path to Beck Head bears to L. A conspicuous erect boulder, known as Moses' Finger, protrudes from the side of the mountain some distance above. Scramble up the scree past this, to reach a path at height about 550 m. Bear to R here and follow the path, the south Gable traverse, which passes below the White Napes and the Great Napes, but at Little Hell Gate, between these two buttresses, turn to L up the scree and hug its retaining wall on R. After

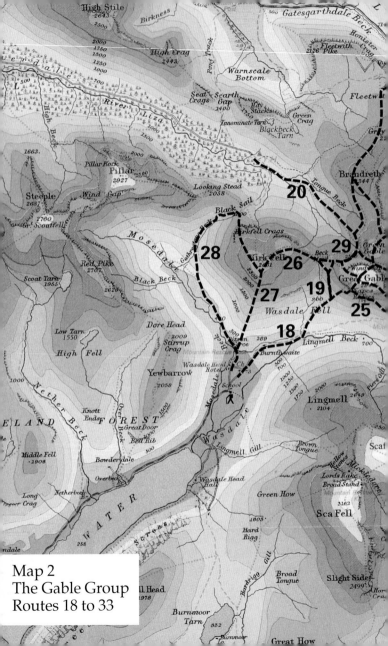

Map 2
The Gable Group
Routes 18 to 33

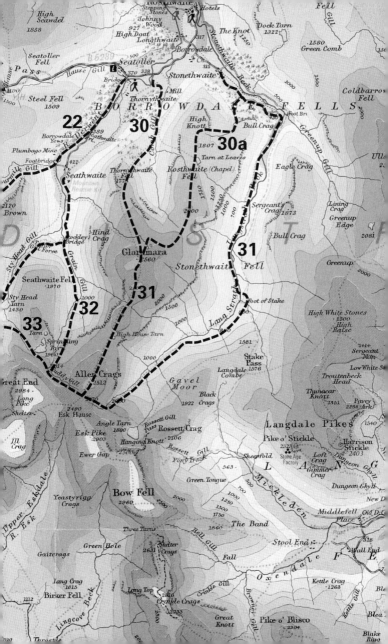

some distance the Sphinx (or Cat) Rock is seen on R, above the Climbers' Traverse path. Follow this path for a short distance for the best view of the Sphinx Rock. A gully will be noticed as the first rift in the crags high up on L, just after the Sphinx is passed. Ascend this until the crest of the Sphinx Ridge is gained and then scramble up this airy escarpment, which merges with the Arrowhead Ridge just below the Great Napes summit. This reveals Westmorland Crags, with a large cairn, which shield the summit of Gable. While experienced climbers may reach this belvedere by devious routes up the face of the shattered cliff ahead, it is safer for the pedestrian to keep to a path which skirts them on L and so avoid all difficulties.

Considering the importance of Great Gable, the cairn on its summit is scarcely as imposing as it might well be. It has, however, a greater intrinsic interest than any other of the Lakeland summits, for a tablet in the north face of the summit boulder marks the presentation to the National Trust of this and other adjacent peaks in memory of those members of the Fell and Rock Climbing Club who fell in the First World War, 1914–18.

The panorama from this mountain is magnificent and reveals the distant fells in all directions, excepting to the south, where the higher Scafell massif blocks the view and forms a wild and impressive group beyond Sty Head Pass far below. To R of it, Illgill Head and Yewbarrow together cradle Wastwater backed by the sea in the vicinity of Seascale. Pillar rises superbly above the extensive plateau of Kirk Fell to the west, but the High Stile group on its R is not seen to advantage beyond the trench of Ennerdale. The Grasmoor fells, however, afford the most striking prospect to the north-west, with the noble form of Skiddaw rising to their R above Dale Head. Blencathra stands in splendid isolation on the north-eastern horizon, and then the whole of the Helvellyn range occupies the eastern skyline, well above the intervening ridges. The Langdale Pikes are promi-

Sty Head

Napes Ridges

Beck Head

Plate 37 **Routes 18** and **19** on Great Gable, seen from Down in the Dale

nent in the south-east beyond the long ridge of Glaramara and the light glints on the waters of Sprinkling Tarn almost immediately below Esk Hause, where the path rising to it from Sty Head may be clearly perceived.

Route 19. Wasdale, Gavel Neese and Beck Head. Follow Route 18 to below Moses' Finger, and then take the path across the scree to L. This emerges at Beck Head near the smaller of two tarns. Walk on to the small eminence beyond it on R and then scramble up the steep shoulder on to the summit, keeping the precipices of Gable Crag well on L.

Route 20. Ennerdale and Windy Gap. From Black Sail Youth Hostel in Ennerdale, looking to the south-east, a spur, Tongue, will be observed running up to Green Gable, with Tongue Beck on L, and the stream descending from Windy Gap on R. Make for the foot of this escarpment by crossing the moraine heaps which are a conspicuous feature hereabouts. Ascend south-eastwards on path traces on Tongue, to a wide path, Moses' Trod, reached at height 630 m, GR 211112. Bear to R along this path to the stream below Stone Cove, where turn south-east on a path. The fine shadowed precipices of Gable Crag rise on R, and on attaining Windy Gap turn sharp to R and ascend the path which keeps above them until the summit of the mountain is reached.

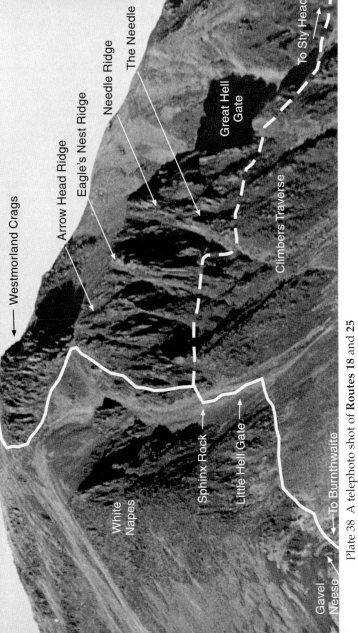

Westmorland Crags

Arrow Head Ridge

Eagle's Nest Ridge

Needle Ridge

The Needle

Great Hell Gate

To Sty Head

Climbers Traverse

White Napes

Sphinx Rock

Little Hell Gate

To Burnthwaite

Gavel Neese

Plate 38 A telephoto shot of **Routes 18** and **25**

Westmorland Cairn →

Napes Summit

Plate 39 **Route 18**—There are other variations for the rock climber

Plate 40 **Route 18**—Westmorland Cairn from below,
Langdale Pikes in the distance

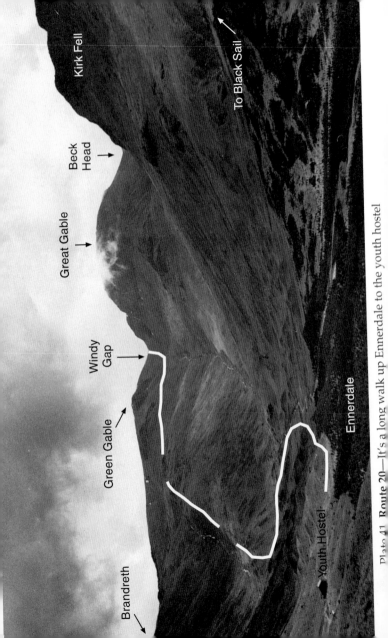

Plate 41 **Route 20**—It's a long walk up Ennerdale to the youth hostel

Route 21. Honister Hause and Green Gable. Walk a short way along the quarry road heading for Honister Crag, and then bear L along the dismantled tramway path, to the ruins of the Drum House at GR 216135. Bear to L along the prominent path which skirts Grey Knotts and passes to the west of Brandreth. Be careful to follow the correct path, L, at the junction at GR 213126, west of Grey Knotts summit. Hereabouts the views to R along both the Buttermere and Ennerdale valleys are magnificent and reveal the well-known lakes of Buttermere and Crummock Water in the former and Ennerdale Water in the latter, with the High Stile group of hills rising between them. The path bends to L as far as some small tarns at Gillercomb Head and then ascends southwards to Green Gable. After lingering here to admire the splendid view of Gable Crag and the vista down Ennerdale which is dominated by Pillar, descend to Windy Gap and follow Route 20 to the summit of Great Gable.

High Stile

Grasmoor

Buttermere Valley

Brandreth

Haystacks

Green Gable

Plate 42 **Route 21**—The view from Green Gable

Plate 43 **Route 22**—Base Brown dominates the approach to Sourmilk Gill

Plate 22. An oblique view of the Gill

Route 22. Seatoller and Gillercomb. The road to Seathwaite diverges to L just below Seatoller. It crosses a bridge spanning Hause Gill and a kilometre further on reaches Seathwaite Bridge. Take the path on R of the bridge which goes beside the river and passes below the famous Borrowdale Yews to a footbridge at the foot of Sourmilk Gill, whose cascades are a prominent feature in wet weather. This is the more beautiful approach but is longer than that which starts under the arch of the farm buildings in Seathwaite. Take the popular zigzag path up the steep slopes on the L of the stream. This enters the spacious hanging valley of Gillercomb, where Gillercombe Buttress is a conspicuous feature of Raven Crag on the R; it is actually on the east face of Grey Knotts and is one of the local playgrounds for the rock climber. The path keeps to L of the hollow, gradually rising across the flanks of Base Brown to emerge in a zigzag on the hause south-west of Base Brown. Ascend the path south-west to Green Gable. Route 21 then leads to the summit of Great Gable.

An alternative on entering Gillercomb is to keep to the ridge of Base Brown all the way to the hause and has the advantage of the views disclosed by this fine fell, but this variation involves the long, rough and continuously steep ascent of some 530 m (1750 ft) from Seathwaite.

Plate 45 **Routes 23** and **24** take a sharp rise here

Route 23. Seathwaite, Sty Head and Aaron Slack. From the hamlet of Seathwaite keep to the broad stony track with the river on ʀ as far as Stockley Bridge, and then after passing through a gate ascend the steep hillside ahead, passing through another gate to where the path skirts the conifers enclosing Taylorgill Force. A large cairn here marks the 1000 ft contour and reveals the path ahead in the deeper confines of the pass with the stream coming down on ʀ. Cross the footbridge, and as soon as Styhead Tarn comes into view ahead bear to ʀ and pick up the path by the beck descending from Aaron Slack. Ascend this wild ravine as far as Windy Gap and then turn ʟ to ascend to the summit of Gable.

Route 24. Sty Head and the Breast Route. Follow Route 23 to Styhead Tarn. Pass to the ʀ of it and continue on the path to the Mountain Rescue stretcher box at GR 219095. Sty Head may also be reached from Wasdale Head by the path across the south flank of Great Gable. From the stretcher box follow the reconstructed path north-west up the breast of Gable, and continue further on the path to the summit cairn.

Route 25. Sty Head and the Climbers' Traverse. Follow Route 24 to the stretcher box at Sty Head Pass. Find a path heading westwards, to the L of the Breast Route path. Walk along it into the recess at the foot of Kern Knotts. This imposing crag is unmistakable, and rock climbers may often be seen ascending one or other of the cracks on its face. Scramble down the maze of large boulders on L, and skirt the buttress to reach the continuation of the path. This rises across the flanks of Great Gable and reveals splendid views down on L into Wasdale. Some distance higher up it passes another outcrop of rocks where a spring is hidden beneath the overhanging crags on R; this is the last place where a drink may be obtained on this route. Cross the wide exit of Great Hell Gate a short way ahead and ascend the narrow path below Tophet Bastion which rises superbly on R. When it bifurcates keep to the right-hand branch which leads into Needle Gully, because if you follow the left branch, the south Gable Traverse, it goes below the Great Napes and joins route 18 at Little Hell Gate. Scramble up Needle Gully as far as the Napes Needle, which stands high up on R, and ascend the rock staircase on L (facing the Needle) which leads to the Dress Circle. This ledge is situated immediately below the gigantic wall supporting Eagle's Nest Ridge and is well named. Then traverse the ledge carefully round the corner, and squeeze through a narrow gap behind a flake of rock which gives access to Eagle's Nest Gully. There is an awkward step down the corner R into it (see Plate 52), and then the route passes below Arrowhead Ridge to the Sphinx Rock. Follow Route 18 for Great Gable summit.

Scafell Pike

Lingmell

Lingmell Col

Sty Head

To Esk Hause

Sty Head Tarn

Plate 46 **Route 23**—This tarn is often frozen in winter

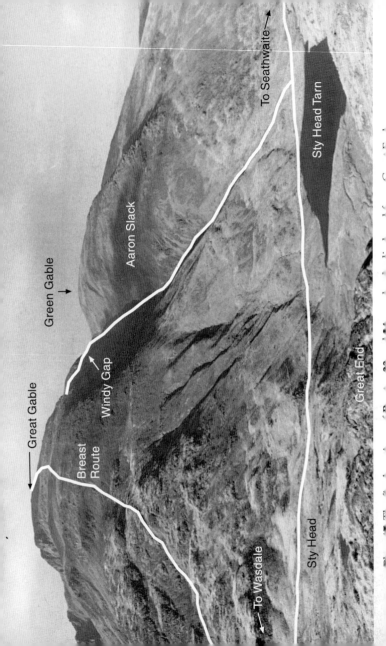

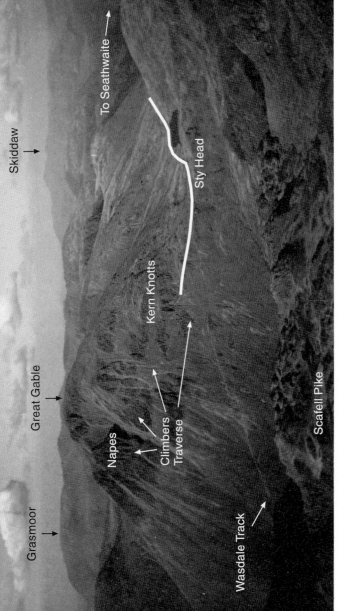

Plate 48 A spacious prospect of **Route 25**

Innominate Crack

Kern Knotts Crack

Climbers Traverse

Plate 49 The popular rock climbs on Kerns Knotts

Eagles Nest Ridge

Abbey Buttress

Eagles Nest Gully

Needle Ridge

Napes Needle

Napes Traverse

Plate 50 The Napes Ridges

Plate 51 **Route 25**—Climbing Napes Needle

Plate 52 On the Climbers Traverse

Plate 53. The view from the Gable to Buck

Illgill Head

Screes

Wastwater

Yewbarrow

Sphinx
Rock

Gable

Wasdale

Lingmell

Plate 54 North-west from Gable

Blencathra   Clough Head   Great Dodd

Gillercombe Buttress

Great Gable

Plate 55. North-east from Gable

Kirk Fell

Route 26. Wasdale and Beck Head. Follow Route 19 to Beck Head. The path to Kirk Fell leaves the larger of the two tarns here and rises via Rib End to the two tops, at 787 m and 802 m, on the vast plateau. The best views are obtained from its eastern rim, which reveals an unusual prospect of Great Gable to the east, and by evening lighting a beautiful panorama of the Scafells, which rise above the nearer eminence of Lingmell to the south-east.

Route 27. From Wasdale direct. From near the Wasdale Head Inn take the track past the packhorse bridge and Row Head to the open fell. Follow the path which rises steeply up the grassy spur of Kirk Fell straight ahead. Keep to the spur and there is a path most of the way to the summit cairn. This is a continuously steep and trying ascent.

Route 28. Wasdale and Black Sail Pass. From near the Wasdale Head Inn take the track past the packhorse bridge and Row Head to the open fell. Take the path on L which keeps to the stone wall for some distance. It afterwards bears to R and skirts the flanks of Kirk Fell as far as Gatherstone Beck, with fine views to L into the spacious hollow of Mosedale. Cross the stream and ascend the steeper path to the top of Gatherstone Head, which discloses its further course swinging round to R to the col on the skyline. This is Black Sail Pass, and from its summit turn sharp to R across the rising ground and scramble up the shattered Kirkfell Crags which rise high overhead. Follow the ridge further, past some old fence posts, to the higher summit, 802 m.

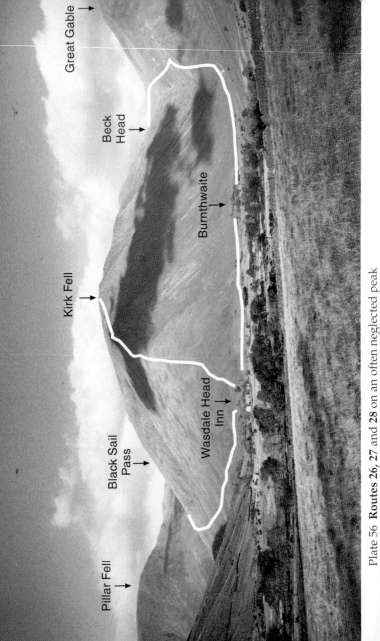

Plate 56 **Routes 26, 27** and **28** on an often neglected peak

Plate 57 **Route 26**—The Scafell Pikes and Lingmell from the summit of Kirk Fell

Plate 58 **Route 26**—Retrospect of the Gables

Plate 59 **Route 26**—The tarns and summit cairns on Kirk Fell

Route 29. Honister Hause and Moses' Trod. Follow Route 21 as far as the slope west of Brandreth summit, then drop down over the grassy flank south, to find a path west of Gillercomb Head. Follow this path, known as Moses' Trod, south to the stream descending from Windy Gap. Now follow it to R, well below Gable Crag on L, where it rises to a small hump, which reveals Beck Head with its two tarns just below. Descend to the col and then follow Route 26, via Rib End, as far as the summit of Kirk Fell.

Plate 60 **Route 30** ends on a fine Lakeland viewpoint

Glaramara

Route 30. Rosthwaite and Thornythwaite Fell. Leave Rosthwaite by the Seatoller road and walk along it as far as Mountain View, just short of the bridge over the River Derwent. Take the farm road L and after a short way a stile gives access to the wooded slopes on L. Pick up the path which rises on the western side of Combe Gill, and on emerging from the trees discloses a fine prospect of the gigantic hollow of The Combe ahead. Take the path bearing to the R, south-west. It follows a sinuous course and skirts many a craggy knoll on the approach to the top of Thornythwaite Fell. Here the view is surprising, for it unfolds a striking prospect of Honister Crag protruding above Honister Pass to the north-west, and also a delightful vista to the north along the green strath of Borrowdale. Gillercomb is revealed on the opposite side of the Seathwaite valley. The bold summit of Glaramara appears almost due south, and you cross the intervening boggy ground in a direct line with it, keeping well away from the precipitous edge above Raven Crag on the L which, however, reveals a remarkable view of Doves' Nest Caves opposite. A pleasant scramble leads to the twin cairns gracing this peak; the near one retrospectively disclosing Derwentwater and Skiddaw beyond Borrowdale, and the far one providing a striking prospect of the Langdale Pikes away to the south-east across the deep trench of Langstrath. The second summit, at 783 m, to the south-west, partially blocks the panorama in this direction, but it is worth while to walk over to it for the view of Great Gable, which rises as a stately giant above the nearer top of Seathwaite Fell. This belvedere, and the third summit, 775 m, south, moreover open up the full-length prospect of the long ridge of Glaramara to the south and reveal the unexpected undulations of its topography as far as Allen Crags, together with the deeply gullied precipitous façade of Great End on R.

Plate 61 **Route 30**—Looking across Combe Gill to Doves' Nest Caves

Plate 62 **Route 30**—Skiddaw and Derwentwater from the summit of Glaramara

Route 30a. Over Rosthwaite Fell. This is a long and circuitous route to Glaramara; it begins at Stonethwaite and should on no account be attempted in dense mist. Follow the track in the direction of Langstrath, and after crossing two streams, Little and Big Stanger Gills, turn uphill into the trees on R and walk up the steep twisting path beside Big Stanger Gill which in its higher reaches crosses an awkward stone wall below Alison-grass Crag on L before attaining a grassy col. Note the magnificent retrospect of Borrowdale below and then follow the gill west, keeping several craggy eminences on L. Visit the cairn at GR 257128, above High Knott, as this opens up a dynamic view of Honister Crag and Seatoller, as well as a splendid vista along Borrowdale to Skiddaw. Then walk south and ascend Bessyboot which discloses a variety of views in all directions, including Tarn at Leaves which is cradled in a grassy basin at its base and backed by the fine profile of Pike o'Stickle. The route ahead is now clear and the next point of interest is the rocky top of Rosthwaite Cam, to the right of which rises Combe Head, with a glimpse of Glaramara on its R; further to R there is also a good view of Raven Crag on the other side of Combe Gill. Walk up the grassy slopes to Rosthwaite Cam and continue ahead to the next eminence, near the head of the ravine of Woof Gill. Beyond this walk up the slopes south-westwards, and pass the opening, Combe Door, on R. Scale Combe Head for the fine view of the gloomy hollow of Combe Gill, with Doves' Nest Caves on R, and then go ahead to Glaramara, whose summit is reached by a pleasant rock scramble.

Plate 63 **Routes 30a, 31, 108 and 109** from Castle Crag

Plate 64 **Route 30a**—Borrowdale and Stonethwaite from Big Stanger Gill

Plate 65. Beinn 28a, Clàidheamh Rìgh, a mountain pass

Plate 66 **Route 30a** passes a tarn that is seldom visited

Tarn at Leaves

Rosthwaite Cam · Comb Head · Glaramara · Raven Crag · Comb Gill · Bessyboot

Plate 67. Route 20a

Route 31. Langstrath and Esk Hause. Leave Rosthwaite by the bridge to Hazel Bank, turn to R, and follow the track by Stonethwaite Beck and across Stonethwaite Bridge to Stonethwaite. Follow the track south-east then bear R on the track through a gate into Langstrath. A footbridge crosses Langstrath Beck. Follow the path up the valley west of the beck, and cross a footbridge to reach a footbridge over Stake Beck at the foot of Stake Pass. An alternative is to use the path east of Langstrath Beck to the foot of Stake Pass. Follow the path traces south-west, keeping Langstrath Beck then Allencrags Gill on R. The path traces accompanied by several small cairns lead steeply to the Angle Tarn/Esk Hause path north-west of Tongue Head. Walk up the path to the hause near the cross-shaped wall shelter, which lies to the north-east of Esk Hause summit. Ascend the path north-east to Allen Crags summit, a fine viewpoint for Great End and Great Gable. Take the path north-east for Glaramara, which passes many lovely small tarns from where there are good views of the Langdale Pikes.

Route 32. Grains Gill and Esk Hause. From Seathwaite follow the track to Stockley Bridge. On the other side turn sharp to L and follow the path near Grains Gill then Ruddy Gill. After crossing Ruddy Gill, above its ravine, and below Great End, take the path south-east for the hause between Esk Hause proper on R and Allen Crags on L. Then follow Route 31 for Glaramara.

Route 33. Sty Head and Esk Hause. Follow Route 24 as far as Sty Head, and at the stretcher box bear to the south-east across swampy ground and pick up the well-cairned path which skirts the lower slopes of Great End. Pass Sprinkling Tarn, ascend the rising ground with Ruddy Gill on L, to join Route 32 north of Esk Hause. Follow the path to the hause south-west of Allen Crags, then follow Route 32 to Glaramara.

Plate 68   The Gables and Pillar from Glaramara

Plate 69 **Route 31**—The Langdale Pikes from High House Tarn

The Pillar Group

Pillar	892 metres	2926 feet
Scoat Fell	841 metres	2759 feet
Red Pike	826 metres	2710 feet
Steeple	819 metres	2687 feet
Haycock	797 metres	2615 feet
Caw Fell	c697 metres	2287 feet
Yewbarrow	628 metres	2060 feet
Black Sail Pass	*549 metres*	*1800 feet*

OS Map: Landranger 89 West Cumbria
              Outdoor Leisure 4 North Western Area
              Outdoor Leisure 6 South Western Area

Pillar
Route 34. Wasdale and the High Level Route. Follow Route 28 to Black Sail Pass summit, and then turn to L along the ridge leading towards Looking Stead, whose top should be visited, for the view. This top may, however, be reached more directly from Gatherstone Head by taking a short cut path up the fellside. Bear to the south-west up the ridge rising to Pillar, but almost immediately, at GR 184117, pick up the High Level Route which diverges to R and provides one of the most spectacular walks in Lakeland. The path undulates along the stony shelf which leads to Robinson's Cairn. This discloses the buttress of Shamrock, and Pillar Rock, one of the most famous climbing grounds in Britain, towards which the path at first descends and then rises to a rocky shelf. Ascend this ledge, the Shamrock Traverse, with care as it rises above the splendid conformation of the Shamrock. Then scramble round the well-marked rocks encircling the stone shoot above Walker's Gully

Plate 70 **Route 34** seen from the Scafell path

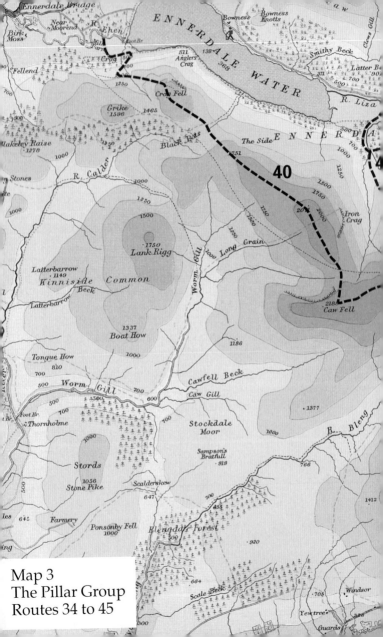

Map 3
The Pillar Group
Routes 34 to 45

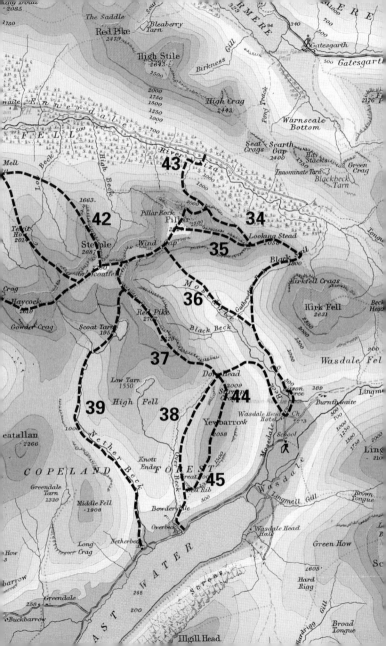

(down on R), to Pisgah. Pisgah is the craggy eminence abutting on the hillside to L of High Man, the upper part of the Pillar Rock complex. Note on R the Slab and Notch Route to High Man.

From the col near Pisgah, a bold ridge leads up the skyline. Ascend this to the top, where the summit of the mountain appears ahead.

Note – Walker's Gully and the Slab and Notch Route are rock climbers' routes only, and *not* for fellwalkers.

The panorama from Pillar is extensive, but scarcely impressive, owing to the flattish top of the mountain. The most striking prospect is to the south-east from Great Gable to Scafell; the former appearing over the vast summit of Kirk Fell and the latter rising splendidly beyond the deep hollow of Mosedale far below. Red Pike, Scoat Fell and Steeple form a high massive group to the south-west and rather block the distant view, but Ennerdale Water may be seen to the west over the long shoulder of the last named. The Grasmoor hills to the north are largely obscured by the barren craggy slopes of the High Stile range on the other side of Ennerdale. Skiddaw and Blencathra rise on the north-eastern horizon above the western peaks of the Dale Head group, while the Helvellyn range bounds the eastern prospect. The most spectacular view, however, is obtained from the edge of the precipices enclosing Great Doup, slightly to the east, where the strangely contorted crags descend in one wild sweep into the depths of Ennerdale, over 600 m (2000 ft) below.

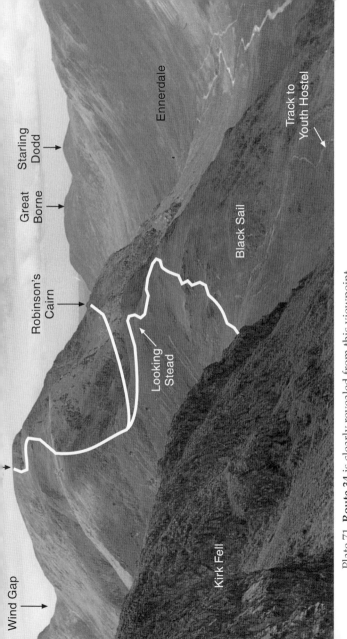

Plate 71 **Route 34** is clearly revealed from this viewpoint

Wind Gap

Robinson's Cairn

Great Borne

Starling Dodd

Ennerdale

Track to Youth Hostel

Black Sail

Looking Stead

Kirk Fell

Plate 72. Route 24. Fell walkers on the High Level Route.

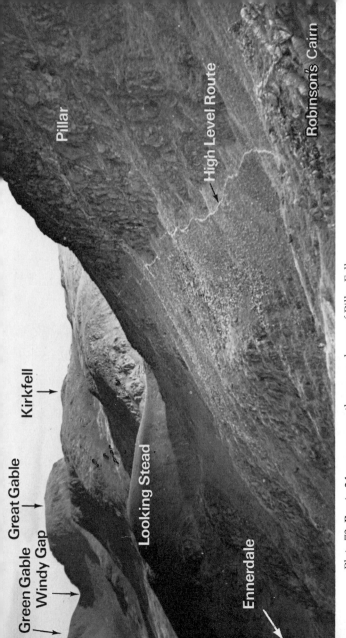

Plate 73 **Route 34** runs across the scree slopes of Pillar Fell

Plate 71. **Route 24.** The east face of Pillar Rock from Robinson's Cairn; the track continues up...

Plate 75 **Route 34**—Pisgah and High Man; note the climber, centre, on Slab and Notch

Plate 76 **Route 34**—Slab and Notch; an easy climb on High
Man

Plate 77 **Route 34**—High Man and Pisgah from the fellside above

Plate 78 The western face of Pillar Rock

Route 35. Wasdale and Pillar. Follow Route 34 to Black Sail Pass, and the start of the High Level Route, and then ascend the ridge path which ultimately leads to the summit of Pillar.

Route 36. Wasdale, Mosedale and Wind Gap. Follow Route 34 until a height of about 160 m is reached, south of Gatherstone Beck, then follow the path traces towards Mosedale Beck. Keep this on L as you walk up the slope north-west, thereafter diverging slightly to R, and ascend the rough and steep hillside then scree shoot straight towards the first gap in the skyline on the left of Pillar. Do not follow the main stream which rises on Scoat Fell. On reaching Wind Gap, bear to R up the rough slope to the summit of the mountain.

Great End → Bowfell → Broad Crag → Scafell Pike → Mickledore → Scafell →

Kirkfell

Lingmell

Summit of Pillar Fell

Route 37. Wasdale, Dore Head and Red Pike. This route is more generally used to terminate the circuit of the 'Mosedale Horseshoe'. Those who wish to use it for the ascent of Pillar, however, may cross the packhorse bridge behind the Wasdale Head Inn to the start of the path. After passing through to the open fell, west of Mosedale Beck, skirt the northern escarpment of Yewbarrow, to a sheepfold below Dorehead Screes. A grass path leads west. Cross the screes rut, and ascend the path south-westwards, to the R (north) of the deeply eroded scree run. When the col of Dore Head is attained, the path on the craggy slopes on R leads up to the summit cairn on Red Pike.

The retrospective view is superb and reveals a wonderful vista of the valley rising to Sty Head where Gable frowns down on one side and Great End rises on the other as a lofty sentinel of the Scafells. The wild rifted aspect of this group as a whole is most impressive.

Continuing in a north-westerly direction, the ridge falls slightly and then rises again to Scoat Fell. The summit of Scoat Fell is, however, away from the path which turns to R and skirts the precipices enclosing Black Comb, over Black Crag top, then falls to Wind Gap. From Wind Gap ascend the rough slope north-east to the summit of Pillar.

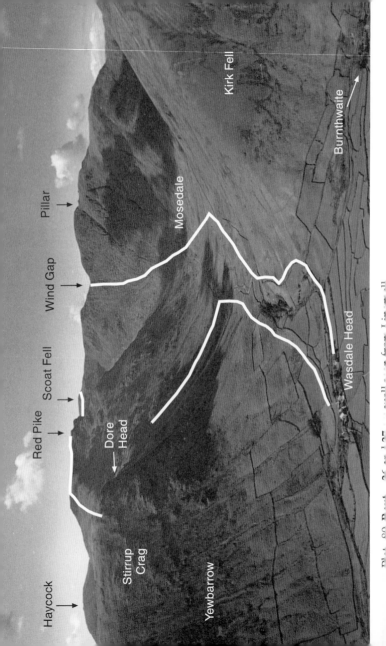

Plate 80. **Pillar**, 26 m (1.25 inches)) screes from Lingmell

Haycock

Stirrup Crag

Yewbarrow

Red Pike

Scoat Fell

Dore Head

Wind Gap

Pillar

Mosedale

Wasdale Head

Kirk Fell

Burnthwaite

Route 38. Overbeck and Red Pike. Overbeck Bridge spans the stream which falls into Wastwater near the terminal slopes of the grand southern spur of Yewbarrow. Follow the path north-eastwards, R of the wall. As the crags are approached, use a stile to cross the wall and follow the path which skirts the crags. Keep to the path, with Over Beck on L, all the way to Dore Head. Then follow route 37 to Pillar.

Route 39. Nether Beck and Scoat Tarn. Netherbeck Bridge is delightfully situated amid the conifers which grace the northern shore of Wastwater below Middle Fell. The stream rises in Scoat Tarn and in its descent forms many pretty cascades, flowing first beneath the craggy slopes of Haycock and Seatallan on the west, and High Fell on the east, and thereafter skirting the lower slopes of Middle Fell before entering the lake. A path ascends by its west bank and affords a charming ascent to Scoat Tarn. From the tarn ascend the slope north-east to the saddle between Red Pike and Scoat Fell. Route 37 then leads to Pillar.

Route 40. Ennerdale Bridge, Haycock and Scoat Fell. This long walk starts at Bleach Green Cottage, GR 085153, east of Ennerdale Bridge and near the foot of Ennerdale Water. Follow the track to behind Crag Farm House, then follow the path east to the lakeshore. Walk up the slopes to Ben Gill, across it, and ascend the steep ground with its ravine on L, until a path is reached above the ravine. Follow this path east-south-eastwards, as it follows a distinctive escarpment. Either cross the flank of Crag Fell south-east to a good track, an old mine road, or take in Crag Fell summit, a good viewpoint at 523 m. In either case the objective is the area of disused mines on the fellside near the junction of walls at the head of Red Beck. Ascend the slope south-east and thereafter keep to the high ground, alongside a wall, above Iron Crag, to a dip at GR 126113. Walk up the fell south then north-east, by the wall to Caw Fell summit, at GR 132110. With the wall alongside continue the ascent by Little Gowder Crag to Haycock summit. Seatallan is conspicuous to the south, while Scoat Tarn appears in the depression to the east. Steeple and Scoat Fell are now prominent to the north-east, and the Scafells make a fine skyline above Yewbarrow to the south-east. The route becomes more interesting as you advance, because you walk along the edge of the crags on the Ennerdale side of Scoat Fell and look down into the wild combes which give birth to Deep Gill and Low Beck. Before reaching Scoat Fell summit, 841 m, it is well worthwhile to make the scramble detour on to the summit of Steeple. From Scoat Fell summit descend east, initially near the stone wall, to join Route 37 to the summit of Pillar.

Route 41. Gillerthwaite, Haycock and Scoat Fell. This route starts at the Ennerdale Forest road at GR 134142, west of Gillerthwaite, at the beginning of the Nine Becks Walk. Cross the footbridge over the River Liza and follow the route of the Nine Becks Walk to the R of Woundell Beck, to reach two footbridges close together, at the confluence of the two main tributaries of Woundell Beck. The first bridge, Friends Bridge, spans Silvercove Beck; the second, over Deep Gill, is Ramblers Bridge. An alternative approach to the two footbridges is by way of the path south from the ford at GR 131142. After crossing the first footbridge, turn R and ascend the path on the tongue between the two streams, to reach the ridge east of Caw Fell summit. Turn L and follow Route 40 over Little Gowder Crag, Haycock and Scoat Fell to Pillar.

Plate 81 **Routes 41** and **42**—Friends Bridge

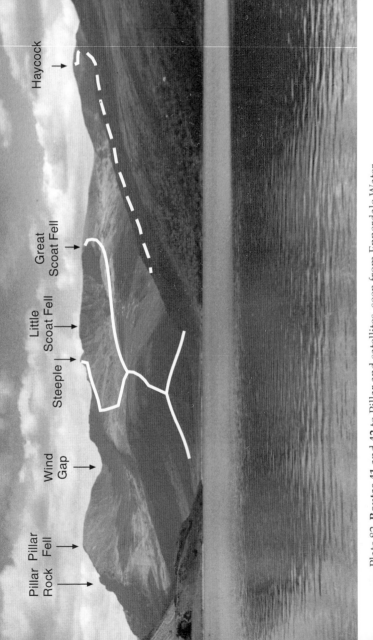

Plate 82 **Routes 41** and **42** to Pillar and satellites, seen from Ennerdale Water

For Scoat Fell direct, cross the second footbridge and ascend the path north-east, to where a grassy firebreak rises from the L. Now ascend the wide break in the trees south-east, a drove way from the open fell of Lingmell. An alternative to the route thus far is to ford Woundell Beck at GR 133138 then walk up the firebreak south to the drove way. From the open fell of Lingmell ascend south-eastwards over Tewit How, to the ridge west of Scoat Fell summit. Turn to L and follow Route 40 for Pillar.

Route 42. Gillerthwaite, Steeple and Scoat Fell. From the Ennerdale Forest road at GR 134142, follow Route 41 to Friends Bridge and Ramblers Bridge. After crossing the two bridges, ascend the path north-east then the drove way south-east on to Lingmell. Cross this fell on path traces in an east-south-east direction to Low Beck. Now pick up a path which rises with Long Crag on L and Mirklin Cove on R to the tiny summit of Steeple. Continue, with scrambling, along the rocky ridge to Scoat Fell, and follow Route 40 for Pillar.

Plate 83 **Routes 41 and 42**—Ramblers Bridge

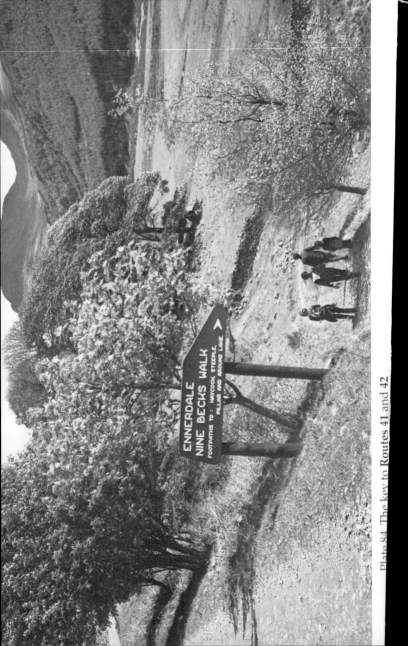

Plate 84 The key to Routes 41 and 42

Plate 85 Steeple—The last stretch of **Route 42**

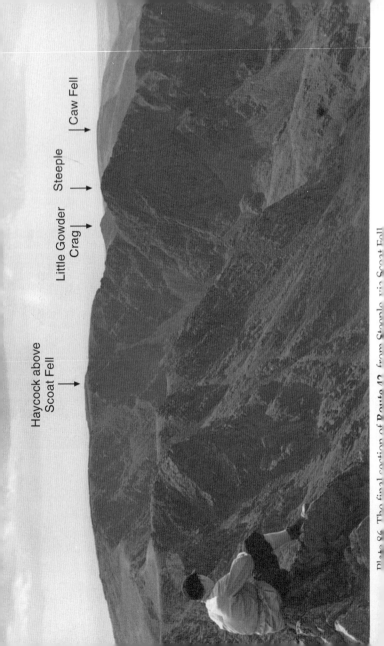

Haycock above Scoat Fell

Little Gowder Crag

Steeple

Caw Fell

Plate 86 The final section of **Route 12** from Steeple via Scoat Fell

F. P. STEEPLE, PILLAR ▶

Plate 87 **Route 41** leaves Nine Becks Walk at this point

Route 43. Ennerdale and Pillar Rock. Pillar Rock rises majest-ically above Ennerdale and is conspicuous throughout the walk up the valley. Walk up the valley forest road from Gillerthwaite to the Pillar Rock War Memorial footbridge at GR 176132. Cross the bridge and turn R along a forest road. From just beyond a road junction, turn L and ascend the break or ride in the trees, with Pillar Rock ahead. From a stile at the forest boundary, at GR 173129, walk up the path close to the beck into the wild combe below the Rock. Now ascend south-east to Robinson's Cairn, thereafter keeping to Route 34 to the summit of Pillar.

Yewbarrow

Route 44. Dore Head and Stirrup Crag. Stirrup Crag is the prominent northern tip of Yewbarrow. Reach it from Wasdale Head by following Route 37 to Dore Head, where it towers overhead on L. Steep crags are encountered here and involve some scrambling before the crest of the ridge is attained, whence the cairn on Yewbarrow summit is reached by walking along the ridge.

Route 45. Overbeck and Great Door. From Overbeck Bridge follow the path north-eastwards, R of the wall. As the crags are approached, use a stile to cross the wall and follow the path skirting the crags on L. Ascend the path on R, which rises between Dropping Crag on L, and the lower rocks of Bell Rib on R. Scramble round the upper rocks of the latter on to the crest of the ridge, where Great Door appears immediately below on the south-eastern face of the mountain. Its vertical retaining walls are conspicuous and provide a spectacular foreground for the view to the east, where the head of Wastwa-ter may be seen far below backed by the magnificent crags of the Scafells. Continue the walk along the ridge to Yewbarrow summit. The retrospective vista of Wastwater stretching away to the south-west is magnificent and reminiscent of one of the smaller Norwegian fiords. An alternative route for the descent to the valley is by way of Dore Head. The descent of the gully of Great Door is not advisable since this route emerges on steep scree and heather.

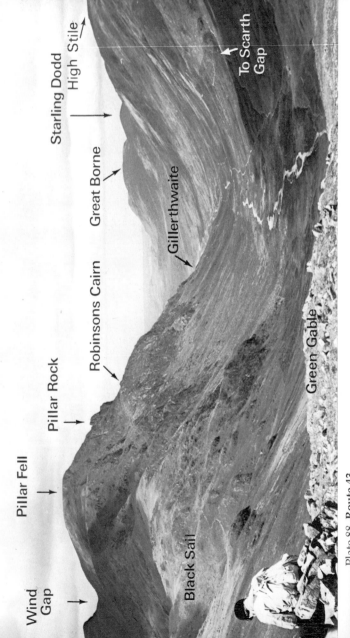

Wind Gap · Pillar Fell · Pillar Rock · Robinsons Cairn · Starling Dodd · High Stile · Great Borne · Gillerthwaite · Black Sail · Green Gable · To Scarth Gap

Plate 88 Route 43

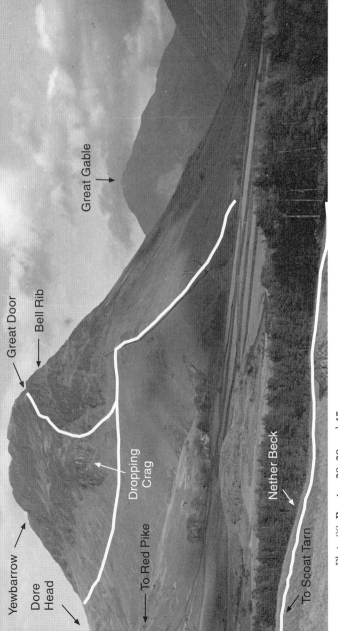

Plate 89 **Routes 38, 39 and 45**

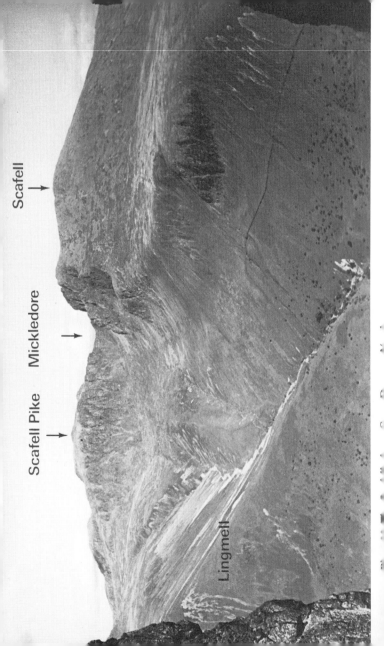

Scafell

Mickledore

Scafell Pike

Lingmell

The High Stile group

High Stile	807 metres	2648 feet
Red Pike	755 metres	2477 feet
High Crag	744 metres	2441 feet
Fleetwith Pike	648 metres	2126 feet
Starling Dodd	633 metres	2077 feet
Great Borne	616 metres	2021 feet
Haystacks	597 metres	1959 feet
Scarth Gap	*427 metres*	*1400 feet*

OS Map: Landranger 89 West Cumbria
 Outdoor Leisure 4 North Western Area

High Stile

Route 46. Buttermere and Scale Force. Take the track to L of the Fish Hotel, then take a track which branches R to Scale Bridge, which is delightfully situated at the foot of the wooded slopes of Red Pike. Turn to R along the stony path which passes near the head of Crummock Water, then continues north-west to near three prominent holly trees, at GR 159171. Here the path rises south-westwards for about 100 m, before rising gently to the footbridge below Scale Force. If the stream is not in spate the cavernous recesses of the ravine may be entered for a close view of the fall. Ascend the path, initially well pitched, on the L (east) of the beck. There is a choice of two paths ascending south-eastwards from the beck. The first path starts with a well-eroded section at height about 310 m, while the second, a wide path, leaves Scale Beck at height about 370 m. Use either to approach Lingcomb Edge. The tip of Red Pike soon appears ahead and may be attained by a direct ascent.

A pile of stones marks the summit of this ruddy peak and

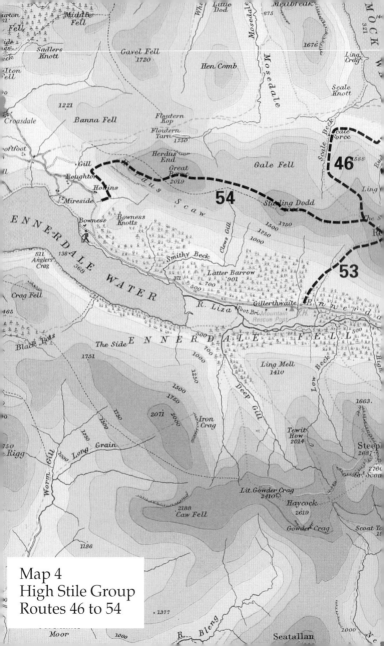

Map 4
High Stile Group
Routes 46 to 54

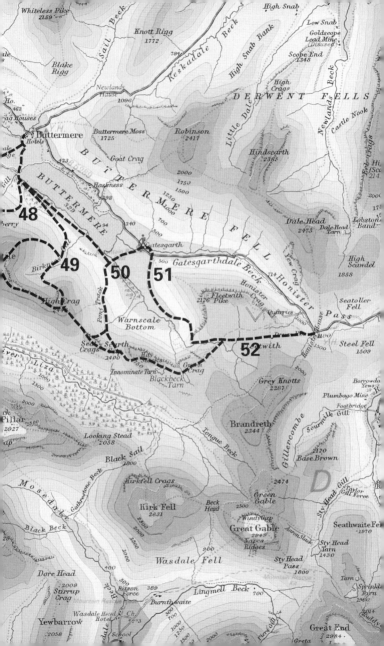

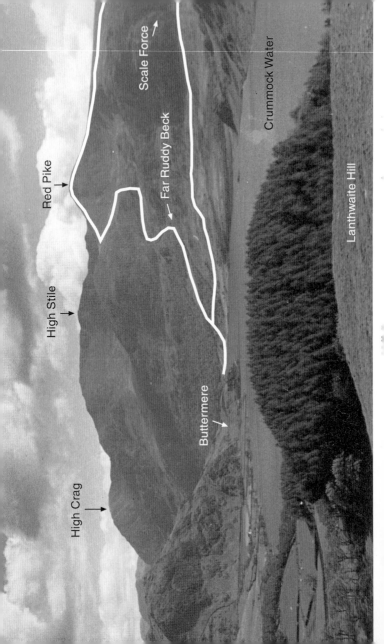

Scale Force

Crummock Water

Far Ruddy Beck

Red Pike

High Stile

Lanthwaite Hill

High Crag

Buttermere

unfolds an impressive vista to the north where Crummock Water lies cradled far below in the vast basin between Mellbreak on L and Grasmoor on R. This view contrasts admirably with the prospect to the south-east which discloses to advantage the wildly rifted north face of Pillar, together with a glimpse of the Scafells on the distant horizon between it and High Stile. The summit of High Stile, the reigning peak of the group, may be attained by a delightful walk along the edge of Chapel Crags which reveals Bleaberry Tarn and Buttermere far below, backed by the Grasmoor hills away to the north.

The panorama from High Stile is magnificent and particularly so to the south-east, where the whole skyline is resplendent with familiar tops from the Langdale Pikes to Great Gable and the Scafells. The first-named stand on the horizon above the long shattered ridge ending with High Crag; Great Gable rises superbly at the head of Ennerdale far below; while the rifted fronts of the last-named completely dominate the scene beyond Kirk Fell and Looking Stead. The valley immediately below stretches away to the right to end with Ennerdale Water, well seen from the west summit (806 m). The gullied façade of Pillar is only seen to advantage by late afternoon light, since at midday it is in shadow. The Grasmoor hills assume a lovely undulating skyline to the north, while the noble forms of Skiddaw and Blencathra close the north-eastern horizon.

Route 47. Buttermere and Far Ruddy Beck. Follow Route 46 as far as Far Ruddy Beck, which descends on L and falls into the head of Crummock Water near a sheepfold. Walk up through the trees, keeping the stream on R, until a path is reached at height about 280 m. An alternative approach to this point is to follow Route 46 to the holly trees at GR 159171, then to ascend south-south-eastwards, initially below a stony, steeper slope, then on a cairned path to Far Ruddy Beck at about 280 m. The path continues through a gap in a stone wall before turning west back towards the beck. Now ascend the path south-south-east then south-east to The Saddle, which lies between Red Pike and the subsidiary eminence of Dodd. Ascend the steep slope south-west by a path to Red Pike summit, then follow Route 46 to High Stile summit.

Route 48. Buttermere and Sourmilk Gill. This stream is a conspicuous white ribbon when seen from the village and rises in Bleaberry Tarn to fall into the foot of Buttermere, where its waters enter the river for Crummock Water. A track from near the Fish Hotel meanders down to this corner of Buttermere and crosses the river by a footbridge, which gives access to Burtness Wood with Sourmilk Gill descending in a wild ravine on R. Do not ascend this ravine, since there is much unsafe ground – in fact there is no safe ascent route here. Route 48 continues by the path rising diagonally through the wood. On emerging from the wood, it zigzags steeply up a scree slope, and on reaching a few wind-blown pines bears to R over a shelf towards Sourmilk Gill. Take the path on the L of the gill, or cross the gill to a path near a wall. The former visits the foot of Bleaberry Tarn. Now ascend the reconstructed path westwards, with Bleaberry Tarn low down on L as you rise to The Saddle, whence Route 47 is followed to Red Pike, and further for the summit of the reigning peak.

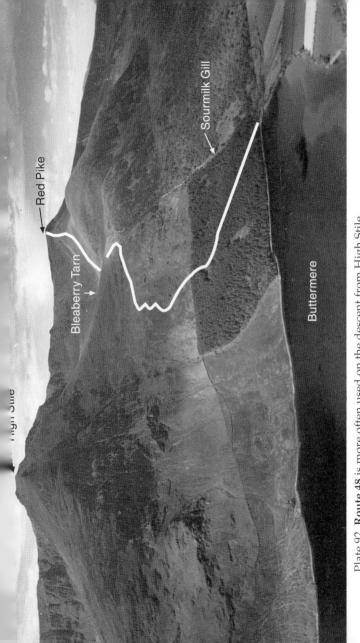

Plate 92 **Route 48** is more often used on the descent from High Stile

Red Pike

Sourmilk Gill

Bleaberry Tarn

Buttermere

High Stile

Plate 92, Route 48 — High Stile opens up some fine views

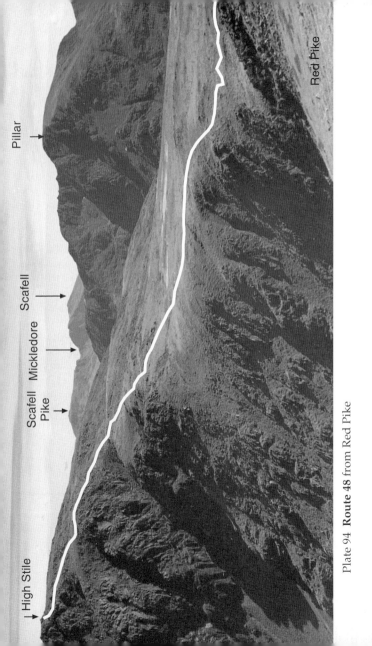

← High Stile   Scafell Pike   Mickledore   Scafell   Pillar

Red Pike

Plate 94 **Route 48** from Red Pike

Route 49. Buttermere and Burtness (Birkness) Comb. Take the track to the foot of Buttermere, then find a track rising south-eastwards, between the lakeside track on L and the path for Bleaberry Tarn and Red Pike on R (Route 48). Continue on the track, bearing to R to finish on a path which reaches the edge of Burtness Wood at a stile, GR 179156. Continue on the path south-east, on the fellside below some low crags, then southwards west of a wall. Ahead is the vast hollow of Burtness or Birkness Comb, which is encircled by many fine but shattered crags. A path leads north-west then west on to the ridge on R. Follow the path on this ridge south-west to High Stile, whose top is more extensive than may be supposed.

High Crag may also be ascended from the floor of the Comb by first crossing Comb Beck and then making for a conspicuous ledge, Sheepbone Rake, high up on L. From the top of this rake, turn R, south, for the cairn on High Crag summit. This reveals a magnificent prospect of Great Gable and the Scafells with the head of Ennerdale far below. A clearly marked path keeps to the crest of the ridge connecting High Crag with High Stile. It skirts the edge of the precipices overlooking Burtness Comb on R and discloses many of the striking buttresses and gullies which characterise the enclosing walls of this great hollow. Grey Crag is the last and most prominent of the buttresses, and after passing it, well to its L, the path rises amid the boulders to the cairn crowning High Stile, which, however, is not perceived until it is almost reached.

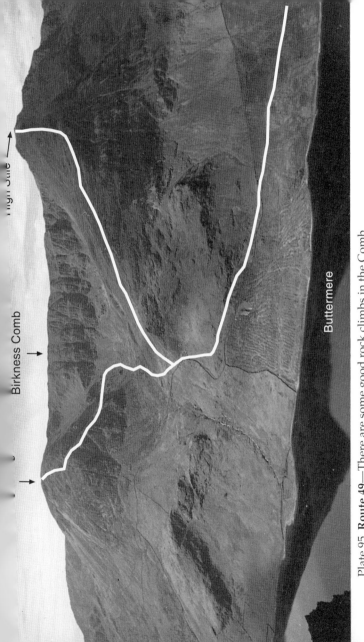

High Stile →

← Birkness Comb

Buttermere

Plate 95 **Route 49**—There are some good rock climbs in the Comb

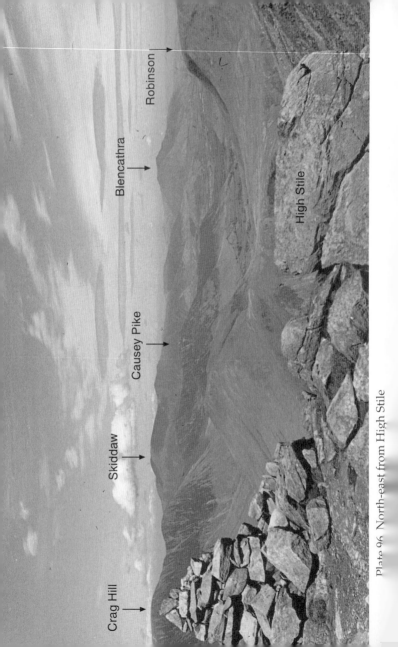

Plate 96 North-east from High Stile

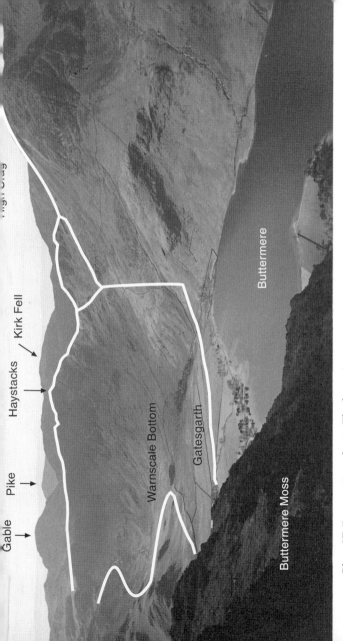

Plate 97 **Routes 50 and 51**—The latter is more picturesque

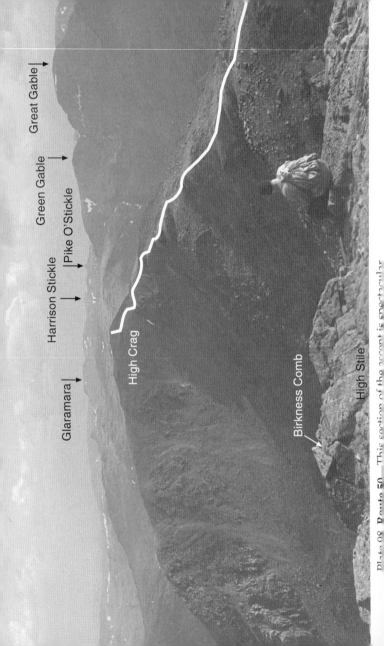

Great Gable

Green Gable

Pike O'Stickle

Harrison Stickle

Glaramara

High Crag

Birkness Comb

High Stile

Plate 98. **Route 50.** This section of the ascent is spectacular

Route 50. Buttermere and Scarth Gap. This pass is well known as providing the connecting link between Buttermere and Ennerdale. It lies between Haystacks and High Crag. It may be attained either by taking the lakeside path through Burtness Wood to the head of Buttermere, where the path rises across the hillside on R straight up to Scarth Gap, or by leaving the Honister Pass road at Gatesgarth and taking the path leading to the footbridge over the stream in Warnscale Bottom and so joining the other path. High Crag towers overhead on R and is reached by following the ridge path over Seat from the top of the pass. A popular short cut goes up by a stone wall on R short of the top of the pass. This skirts the base of Seat and then joins the route on the ridge at the foot of Gamlin End. This provides a steep ascent on scree before the summit is attained. Follow the ridge route described under Route 49 for the summit of High Stile.

Haystacks

Route 51. Warnscale Bottom and Haystacks. Leave the Honister Pass road at Gatesgarth by a path which skirts the flanks of Fleetwith Pike and rises well above Warnscale Bottom. When the ravine of Warnscale Beck is encountered, at 320 m, follow the path continuation to L, beside it, until the old Dubs Quarry workings are reached. Fellwalkers wishing to take in **Fleetwith Pike**, for the beautiful vista of the Buttermere valley, should ascend Fleetwith Edge from Gatesgarth and descend from the summit cairn south-eastwards to the old quarry workings. From Dubs Quarry cross the beck, and keep to the path, which initially passes the foot of Little Round How on L. The small eminence of Green Crag rises ahead, and after it has been passed Blackbeck Tarn appears below. Descend a short section of reconstructed path, across Black Beck, and pick up the rough path on R which heads for the final slopes of Haystacks. On attaining the plateau, Innominate Tarn is at once disclosed, and its setting is the delight of all who see it. Walk along the path west which then ascends the ground north-west to Haystacks summit, with its two cairns and small tarn alongside to the west. The summit reveals High Crag on the other side of Scarth Gap some 150 m below. Scramble down the path on the rough slopes and then follow Route 50 to High Stile.

Route 52. Honister Hause and Haystacks. Walk a short way along the quarry road heading for Honister Crag, and then bear L along the dismantled tramway path, via the ruins of the Drum House, at GR 216135, to Dubs Quarry. Here join Route 51 for Haystacks and High Stile.

High Stile
Route 53. Gillerthwaite and Red Pike. A path leaves the Ennerdale forest road by a gate at GR 146141, east of High Gillerthwaite. It crosses Gillflinter Beck then bears to R over the rough grassy slopes of Red Pike. Ascend these north-eastwards for the summit of the mountain, then follow Route 46 to High Stile.

Route 54. Ennerdale and Starling Dodd. From the road corner at GR 110159 between Routen Farm and Bowness, follow a path north-east to Rake Beck. Ascend the path north-westwards, past a wall corner. Walk up the fellside north-east, with a fence on L, then ascend the ridge path south-east on to the plateau of Herdus. Cross this and make the short ascent east to Great Borne summit. Then keep to the high ground across the depression to Starling Dodd, from where the ridge continues to Little Dodd and Lingcomb Edge. Follow Route 46 from here to Red Pike and High Stile.

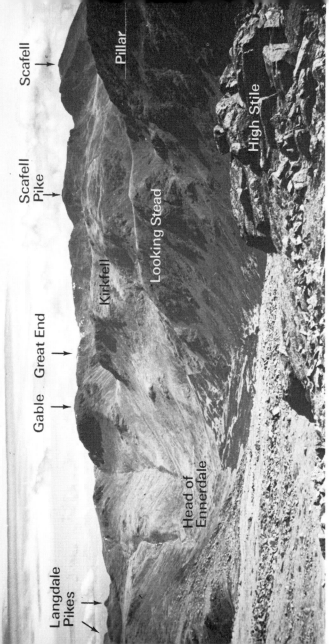

Scafell · Scafell Pike · Kirkfell · Pillar · Gable · Great End · Langdale Pikes · Head of Ennerdale · Looking Stead · High Stile

Plate 99 South-east from High Stile—a marvellous panorama

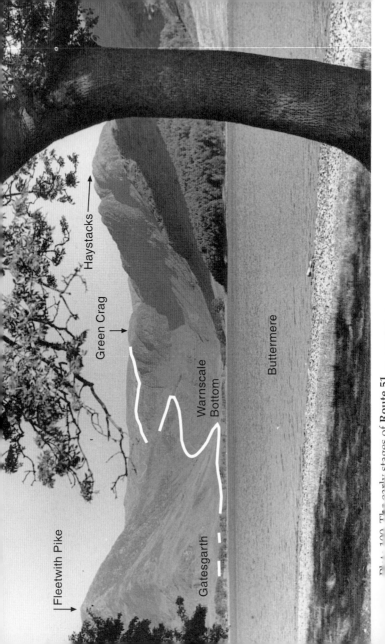

Fleetwith Pike → | Green Crag → | Haystacks →

Buttermere

Warnscale Bottom

Gatesgarth

Plate 100 The early stages of **Route 51**

Plate 101 **Route 52** from Fleetwith

Plate 102 **Route 51**—The Gables from Black Beck Tarn

Plate 103 **Route 51**—Pillar Fell from the Innominate Tarn

Plate 104 **Route 51**—The summit tarn of Haystacks. Grasmoor fells in the distance

The Dale Head Group

Dale Head	753 metres	2470 feet
Robinson	737 metres	2418 feet
Hindscarth	727 metres	2385 feet
High Spy	653 metres	2142 feet
Maiden Moor	576 metres	1890 feet
High Snockrigg	526 metres	1725 feet
Cat Bells	451 metres	1480 feet
Newlands Hause	*333 metres*	*1093 feet*

OS Map: Landranger 89 West Cumbria
   Outdoor Leisure 4 North Western Area

Dale Head

Route 55. Rosthwaite and Dalehead Tarn. Enter the narrow, walled road opposite the shop at Rosthwaite, and follow its continuation, a track, past Yew Tree Farm, to the River Derwent. Turn R at the river, cross New Bridge, and then turn L over the first of two small footbridges, close together. Between the footbridges, cross a stile and follow a path to the L of a stream. *En route* there is a stile, another small footbridge, and another stile. Ascend the track westwards, south of Tongue Gill, to a gate, and the open fell. Now ascend the track's continuation, which is close to, and south of, Tongue Gill. From point GR 239153, ascend the path west-south-west to Rigghead Quarries. The path continues through the ruins, and there is a stile across a fence to the hause. From the hause, Dale Head is disclosed on the other side of the intervening basin which cradles Dalehead Tarn. Follow the path south-west, and pass the tarn to its east. Then strike up the boulder-strewn slopes north-west, on a new path, to the edge of the northern façade of the mountain, at GR 226155. From here the path leads above the shattered cliffs to the cairn on the summit.

Map 5
The Dale Head Group
Routes 55 to 62

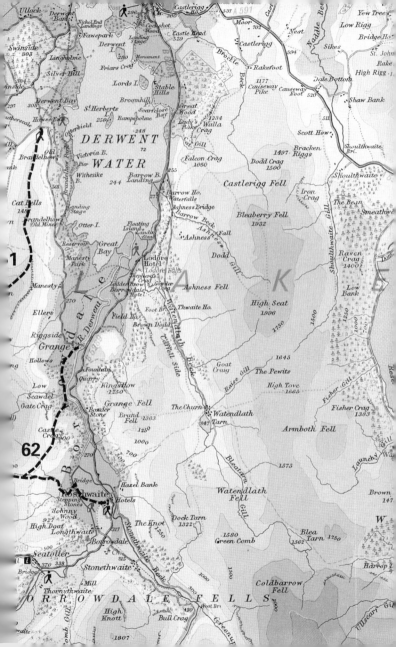

The panorama from Dale Head is noteworthy for the vista along Newlands, which stretches away far below and leads the eye over the Vale of Keswick to rest finally upon the noble form of Skiddaw standing on the northern horizon. The deep valley is hemmed in by the precipices of Eel Crags on R and by the steep slopes of Hindscarth on L, but the distant hills on either side are well seen above them. The view to the south is dominated by Great Gable and the Scafells, which rise above Fleetwith across Honister. They are, however, generally seen in silhouette, unless the walker happens to be on this peak late in the day. The summit ridge narrows considerably to the west of the cairn, and it is hereabouts that the most spectacular views are obtained, since the ground drops away steeply on each side. To the south-west Honister Pass is revealed descending to Buttermere, which is backed by the High Stile range, seen in its entirety.

Route 56. Honister direct. A prominent fence runs up to the north from the crest of Honister Hause. A path which starts on R of the fence leads directly to the cairn on Dale Head. The route is deceptively long, but there are many compensations, not least of which is the grand view of Honister Crag on L.

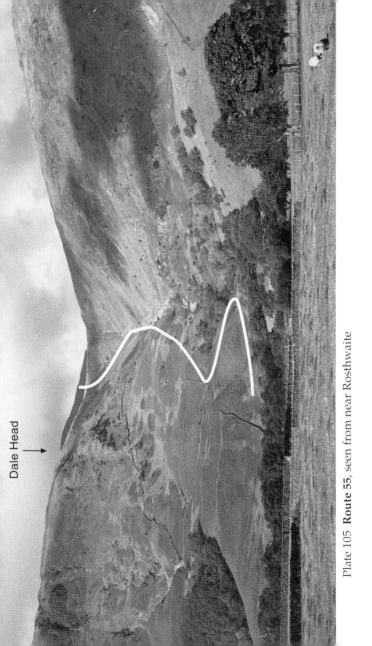

Dale Head →

Plate 105 **Route 55**, seen from near Rosthwaite

Hindscarth

To Newlands Beck

Dale Head

Tarn

Plate 106 Final section of **Route 55**

Plate 107 **Route** 55 reveals the finest view of Eel Crags

High Stile — Red Pike — Great Borne — Dale Head

Plate 108. Borrowdale greywacke, exposure at the westernmost part of the ridge.

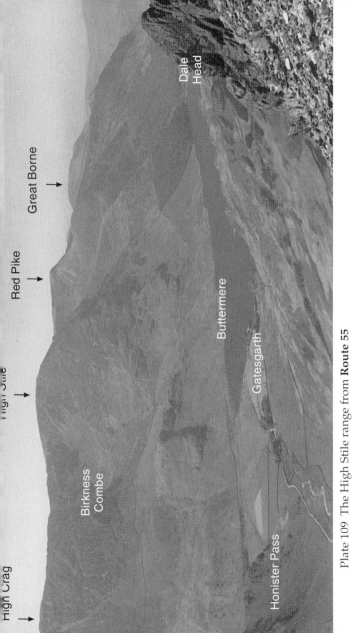

High Crag

High Stile

Red Pike

Great Borne

Birkness Combe

Buttermere

Gatesgarth

Dale Head

Honister Pass

Plate 109 The High Stile range from **Route 55**

Helvellyn Range

Borrowdale

Summit of Honister

To Dale Head

Plate 111 **Route 56** ascends the long slope on the skyline

Route 57. Buttermere and Robinson. Leave the village by the road leading to Newlands Hause, and a short distance from the road junction ascend the path on R which rises across the western flanks of High Snockrigg. It is well marked and has a wide zigzag before reaching the skyline. This discloses the vast grassy basin where the path takes a direct line for Robinson across Buttermere Moss. It is advantageous to make the detour to High Snockrigg summit, which reveals an amazing aspect of Buttermere far below with High Stile rising majestically in the background. After crossing Buttermere Moss, make direct for the summit of Robinson. The view in the northern arc includes a striking prospect from Grasmoor to Blencathra. Turn back to the south and descend over the shaly top as far as the wire fence which meanders along Littledale Edge. Make the detour to Hindscarth summit, another fine viewpoint, then along Hindscarth Edge to rise finally to the cairn on Dale Head. The whole walk, from Robinson to Dale Head, is easy going and rich in marvellous prospects to the south, yielding a remarkable aspect of Pillar which rises superbly beyond Haystacks and Scarth Gap to the south-west.

Route 58. Newlands and Robinson. Take the road going west from Newlands church. There is a convenient car-park near Chapel Bridge, GR 231194. The road leads to Low High Snab. Continue on the track towards Scope Beck. When the open fell is reached, ascend the slopes on R on to the ridge of High Snab Bank. Go along the ridge and make for the northern escarpment of Robinson. The path rises close to the edge of Robinson Crags. Continue the ascent in a south-westerly direction until the summit is reached. Then follow Route 57 to Dale Head.

Route 59. Newlands and Hindscarth. From Newlands church proceed south to Low Snab. Ascend the path westwards on to the ridge. The path climbs the ridge of Scope End as far as High Crags, where Hindscarth appears ahead. Attain and traverse its summit ridge, finally bearing to L for Hindscarth Edge running up to Dale Head. This route reveals a striking aspect of the long line of shattered cliffs known as Eel Crags which stretch from Maiden Moor nearly as far as Dalehead Tarn, and form the dramatic eastern wall of the Newlands Valley.

Route 60. Newlands Beck and Dalehead Tarn. Follow Route 59 to Low Snab and cross a footbridge to a track east of Newlands Beck. Advance on this track south into the deep recesses of the valley. When just beyond Castle Nook, at GR 227168, pick up the path which rises on L across the scree, finally to emerge at Dalehead Tarn. Then follow Route 55 to the summit of the reigning peak of the group. There is an alternative approach from Little Town, where the track east of Newlands Beck starts.

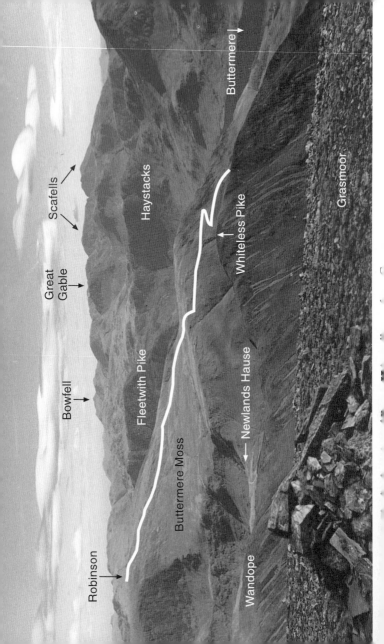

High Stile →   Red Pike →

Robinson

Plate 113 West from Robinson

Eel Crags

Dalehead Tarn

Dale Head

Hindscarth

High Crags

Scope End

Newlands Church

Plate 115 **Route 60** is a gentle ascent

High Spy
Blea Crag
Maiden Moor
Cat Bells
Friar's Crag
Derwentwater

Route 61. Keswick and Cat Bells. A most enjoyable prelude to this walk is to take a launch across Derwentwater to Hawes End. From near Gutherscale, ascend the zigzag path on the grassy northern end of Cat Bells. As height is gained, so the views of the lovely lake below increase in grandeur and reveal more clearly its beautiful setting. The path descends south from Cat Bells summit to Hause Gate. Here the path cuts across the Newlands–Grange path which descends directly to Manesty low down on L. The path continues southwards, and you ascend its uphill course over the grassy top of Maiden Moor. Follow the edge of the precipices on R all the way to High Spy, making only one digression to L to stand by the cairn on Blea Crag. This discloses a most magnificent aspect of Derwentwater. Keep to the crest of Eel Crags, and while noting the fine prospect of Dale Head do not forget the view to the north-west, where the Grasmoor hills, and especially Grisedale Pike, form a grand serrated skyline. Then wander down to Dalehead Tarn, and pick up Route 55 to the summit of its parent peak.

Route 62. Grange and Castle Crag. Leave Grange by the road for Hollows Farm. Take the track past the campsite in Dalt Wood. The track rises to pass through the narrow defile between Castle Crag on the east and the precipitous face of Goat Crag on the west. From just short of the col, a path diverges to L and after crossing a stile and passing through a disused quarry, emerges on the summit of Castle Crag. This is a fine detour from the main route. The main route continues from the col between Goat Crag and Castle Crag as a track which joins Route 55 at Tongue Gill below Rigghead Quarries. Follow Route 55 to Dale Head.

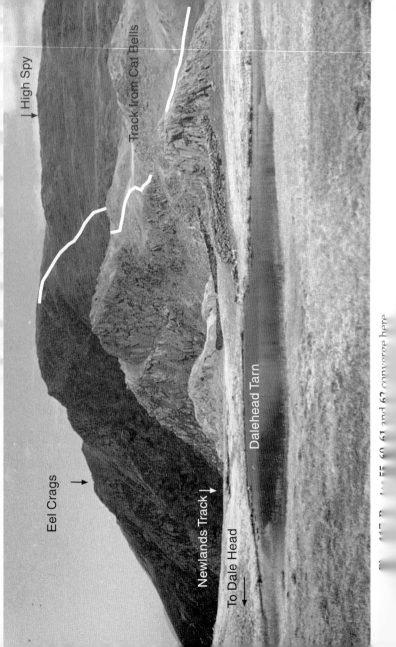

High Spy

Track from Cat Bells

Eel Crags

Newlands Track

Dalehead Tarn

To Dale Head

Paths 59, 60, 61 and 62 converge here

The Grasmoor group

Grasmoor	852 metres	2795 feet
Crag Hill	839 metres	2752 feet
Grisedale Pike	791 metres	2595 feet
Sail	773 metres	2536 feet
Wandope	772 metres	2533 feet
Hopegill Head	770 metres	2526 feet
Whiteside	719 metres	2359 feet
Scar Crags	672 metres	2205 feet
Whiteless Pike	660 metres	2165 feet
Causey Pike	637 metres	2090 feet
Coledale Hause	*610 metres*	*2001 feet*

OS Map: Landranger 89 West Cumbria
　　　　　　Outdoor Leisure 4 North Western Area

Grasmoor
Route 63. Braithwaite and Grisedale Pike. Leave the village by the road to Whinlatter Pass. After a few minutes the end of the old mine road, to Force Crag, is reached at GR 227238. Take the steep path north-westwards from here. The path turns round in a curve, to become a lawn-like path rising along the ridge of Kinn. Grisedale Pike rises ahead with its prominent eastern arête seen end-on. The path takes an oblique line to gain the ridge of Sleet How, whence the eastern arête is gained for the summit of Grisedale Pike.

During the first part of the ascent the retrospective views towards Derwentwater are very beautiful, but the almost parallel ridge from Causey Pike shuts out the scene to the south. From the summit of the mountain the panorama is more extensive round the whole arc, excepting to the south-west, where the great bulk of Grasmoor obscures the distant view.

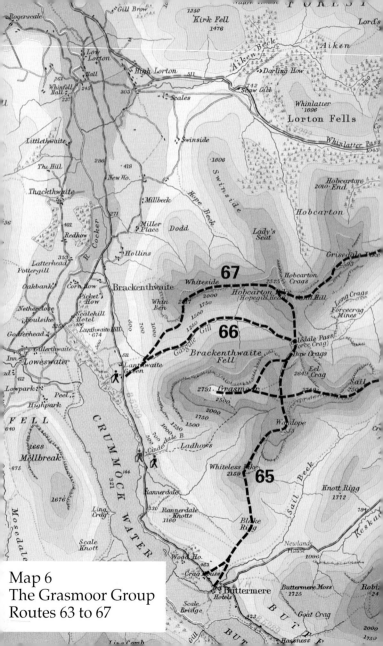

Map 6
The Grasmoor Group
Routes 63 to 67

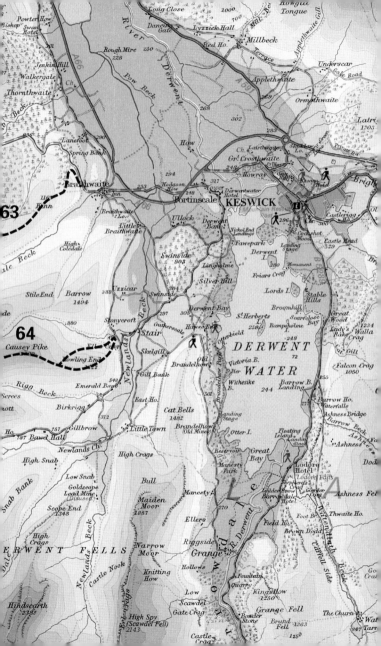

Plate 118. A distant view of the first section of Route 63.

Causey Pike · Sail · Crag Hill · Grasmoor · Coledale Hause · Grisedale Pike · Kinn · Braithwaite · Portinscale · Keswick · Lafrigg

By far the most striking prospect, however, is on the west side, where the shattered cliffs of Hobcarton Crag, on Hopegill Head, present a savage appearance, falling precipitously into the vast intervening combe of the Hobcarton valley.

From Grisedale Pike summit, descend south-westwards on the path which follows a dilapidated stone wall. There is a short ascent to an unnamed summit, height 739 m. From here skirt the edge of Hobcarton Crag, and ascend the path to Hopegill Head summit, a fine viewpoint. Then turn back across Sand Hill, and traverse the col known as Coledale Hause, which is some distance below. Eel Crag rises steeply to the south, but keep it on L and make for the stream coming down from the dip between Crag Hill on L and Grasmoor on R. Either bear up to R up the grassy slopes and follow the edge of Dove Crags, or proceed to the 'dip' referred to above (GR 186202, height 722 m), and ascend the path westwards for Grasmoor. In either case visit the upper edge of Dove Crags, which form the northern boundary of the extensive grassy summit plateau. From here the view is of Brackenthwaite Fell, falling to the ravine of Gasgale Gill. The latter is frowned upon on the north by the seamed flanks of Whiteside. Grasmoor summit is marked by a large cairn west of Dove Crags edge, and close to the edge of the south face of the mountain. From cairns west of the summit, on Grasmoor End, there are views overlooking the foot of Crummock Water, and a bird's-eye view of Loweswater farther to the west.

The panorama from Grasmoor is undoubtedly one of the finest in Lakeland, but to see it at its best it must be observed in the late afternoon of a favourable summer day. At that time the sun is well round to the west when all the peaks engirdling the vast horizon from Skiddaw to Scafell Pike are viewed by the most favourable lighting, and especially the Scafells, which are in silhouette earlier in the day. The succeeding fells to the east, best seen from further east on the summit plateau, afford a wonderful vista, and are backed by the Helvellyn range where Catstye Cam is a conspicuous cone to L of the reigning peak.

From Grasmoor summit, the panorama includes the Langdale Pikes prominent in the south-east, the tip of Pike o'Stickle appearing just to L of the summit of Glaramara. The eye will, however, be attracted by the magnificent array of tops to the south, which stretch across the skyline from Wetherlam on L, over Bowfell and Great Gable, to Scafell Pike and Scafell on R. The higher cairn on Kirk Fell is then disclosed together with a glimpse of Green Crag, seen in the gap between it and Pillar. The last-named rises majestically above the serrated ridge of the High Stile range. Fleetwith Pike and Haystacks look mere insignificant excrescences in the middle distance beyond High Snockrigg and Whiteless Pike, whose western escarpments sink down gracefully to Buttermere and Crummock Water cradled in the narrow valley far below (See Plate 112.)

Route 64. Stair and Causey Pike. From the roadside near the bridge at Stoneycroft, near Stair, strike up the obvious path which rises obliquely across the northern flanks of Rowling End. This is the most direct approach to Sleet Hause which lies at the foot of the sharp arête to Causey Pike, but it may be reached by a more revealing route which diverges to L near Ellas Crag and on attaining Rowling End traverses the full length of the broad ridge with superb prospects on L of Newlands and its enclosing fells. Now ascend the path which goes straight up the ridge of Causey Pike, scrambling up its craggy thimble-shaped top to attain the summit cairn. This reveals the continuation of the path, which keeps to the edge of Scar Crags and then climbs the long grassy slopes of Sail. Cross the fine little ridge which joins it with Crag Hill and descend west-south-west to the hause at GR 186202, at height 722 m. From here pick up Route 63. This ascent is superior to the latter because it affords some grand prospects of the Dale Head group and especially of the deep valleys which penetrate it.

Plate 119 The steepest section of **Route 63**

Grisedale Pike

Eel Crag

Coledale Hause

Sand Hill →

Hopegill Head ↓

Plate 121 **Route 63**—The crags are disclosed at their finest only in early morning

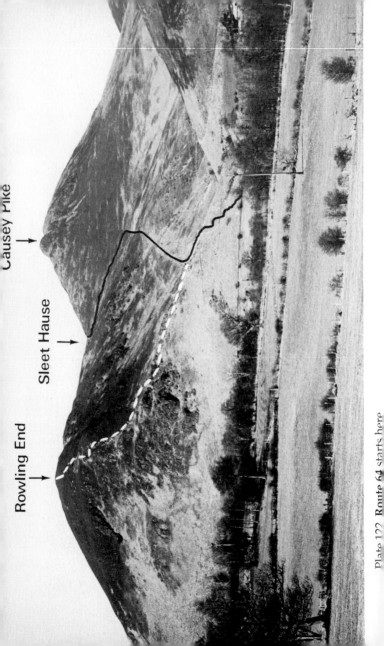

Causey Pike →

Sleet Hause →

Rowling End →

Plate 122 **Route 64** starts here

To Stair

Plate 123 **Route 64** from Sleet Hause ascends the arête to Causey Pike

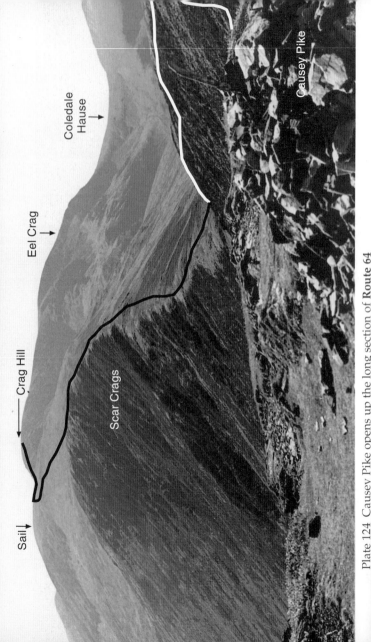

Plate 124 Causey Pike opens up the long section of **Route 64**

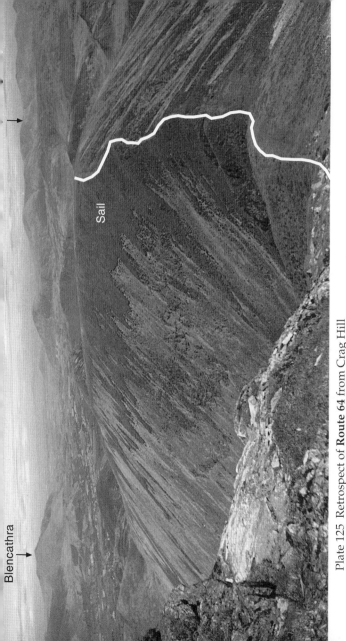

Blencathra

Sail

Plate 125 Retrospect of **Route 64** from Crag Hill

Route 65. Buttermere and Wandope. The usual route leaves the road to Crummock Water at Buttermere Quarry (GR 173172) and rises across the grassy slopes north-eastwards (there are three path variations), but a pleasanter variation is to use the path starting opposite the Bridge Hotel and going through Ghyll Wood, above Mill Beck. In either case, make for the distinctive col at just under 300 m height, at GR 179178. The path then ascends across the slopes of Whiteless Breast and emerges on the grassy shoulder south of Whiteless Pike. The ascent now steepens considerably and reveals increasingly wide retrospective vistas to the south. The ridge, Whiteless Edge, connecting Whiteless Pike with Wandope is narrow with magnificent views down either side. From Wandope summit, descend to the hause at GR 186202 (height 722 m), between Grasmoor and Crag Hill, where Route 63 is picked up for Grasmoor.

Plate 126 **Route 65**

The Location of **Route 65**, seen from High Stile

Grasmoor Cairn at GR 182203

Hause at
GR 186202
(722m)

Plate 128 A close view of the last rise on **Route 65** from a cairn on Whiteless Edge

Route 66. Lanthwaite Green and Gasgale Gill. Lanthwaite Green stands in the very shadow of the great shattered western façade (Grasmoor End) of Grasmoor, an aspect of the mountain that affords some surprise to the newcomer. Whiteside rises to the north, and the wild ravine of Gasgale Gill separates Whiteside from Grasmoor. From the ravine, Liza Beck threads its way ultimately to fall into the River Cocker north of Brackenthwaite. From Lanthwaite Green Farm walk across to the footbridge across Liza Beck. Cross the bridge, and keep to the path on the northern side of the stream, as far as Coledale Hause, whence Route 63 leads to Grasmoor summit.

Route 67. Whiteside and Hopegill Head. From Lanthwaite Green Farm walk across to the footbridge at Liza Beck. Cross the bridge, then bear to L for the path to the eminence of Whin Ben. Thence keep to the crest of the ridge all the way to Whiteside, with spectacular views down into Gasgale Gill on R. After passing the west cairn at 707 m, and the small summit cairn at 719 m, the ridge is narrow and discloses some extensive views to the north over the Solway Firth to the Scottish hills. The ridge drops slightly before Hopegill Head is reached. Continue to Sand Hill, then descend to Coledale Hause, where Route 63 is joined for Grasmoor.

Plate 129 **Route 66** affords a long walk to Coledale Hause

Whiteside →

Grasmoor

Gasgale Gill

Plate 130 Grasmoor yields a spectacular view of Whiteside

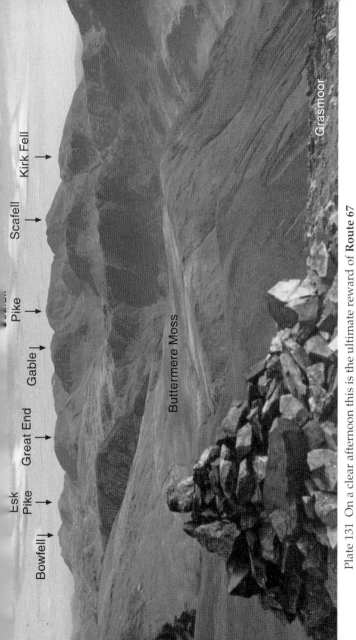

Plate 131 On a clear afternoon this is the ultimate reward of **Route 67**

Bowfell

Esk Pike

Great End

Gable

Pike

Scafell

Kirk Fell

Grasmoor

Buttermere Moss

Skiddaw and Blencathra

Skiddaw	931 metres	3054 feet
Blencathra	868 metres	2847 feet
Little Man	865 metres	2838 feet
Carl Side	746 metres	2447 feet
Latrigg	368 metres	1207 feet

OS Map: Landranger 90 Penrith, Keswick & Ambleside
Outdoor Leisure 4 North Western Area
Outdoor Leisure 5 North Eastern Area

Skiddaw

Route 68. Latrigg and Jenkin Hill. Leave Keswick at the end of Spooney Green Lane, at Briar Rigg (GR 268241). Follow this track, which passes over the A66 road, to the cottages on L and then ascend the well-worn path skirting the western flanks of Latrigg. Follow the zigzag path via Mallen Dodd to Latrigg summit. This divergence from the direct route to Skiddaw is well worthwhile because it unfolds some magnificent prospects to the south and west, which are in fact superior to those revealed from the parent mountain. Walk along the crest of Latrigg to a fence, where Blencathra is fully revealed to the east. Descend northwards, alongside the fence, to the end of Gale Road (GR 281253). The direct route to Skiddaw, i.e. missing out Latrigg, comes in from L (west) here. Cars may be brought to the end of Gale Road. From a stile, take the path for Jenkin Hill, initially between a wall and fence, then past a monument. From here the steepest section of the ascent is displayed. Keep the fence on L and after passing the site of a former refreshment hut, at about 420 m, ascend the path with the wall on R as far as about 620 m; then bear to L and follow the path in a direct line with Little Man. Most walkers traverse

Plate 132 **Route 68** and **69** start from Keswick

Dodd

Ullock Pike

Carl Side

Skiddaw

Jenkin Hill

Latrigg

Spooney Green lane

Millbeck

Keswick

Castle Head

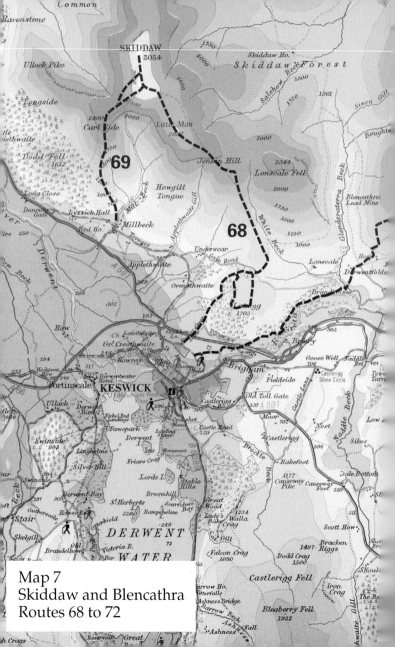

Map 7
Skiddaw and Blencathra
Routes 68 to 72

this subsidiary top, a fine viewpoint, from which descend again to the main path, to the north-west. The main path keeps near the edge of the vast hollow on L and eventually reaches the south cairn on the long summit ridge of Skiddaw. Turn to R along it to attain the highest cairn, with OS column, overlooking the foot of Bassenthwaite Lake. This is not such a good viewpoint as the south cairn, which discloses the immense panorama stretching from Helvellyn in the south-east to Grasmoor in the south-west. Derwentwater is the most conspicuous feature far below which in the sunlight ripples away into the Jaws of Borrowdale and is backed by the majestic fronts of Glaramara and the Scafell range.

Route 69. Millbeck and Carl Side. Millbeck is more famous for the terrace walk along the road connecting it with Applethwaite than as the starting-point for the ascent of Skiddaw. The chief merit of the terrace is its vista to the south over Derwentwater, but its low elevation does not do justice to the scene. This is, however, advantageously viewed from Carl Side, which dominates the hamlet and reveals the lake and dale from approximately the same angle, it being in a direct line with the maximum length of both Derwentwater and Borrowdale. To attain Carl Side, take the path starting at GR 255262. When the open fell is reached, after a short distance, strike up the path on L up the spur of Carl Side (the other path bearing to R gives an alternative approach to Skiddaw via the valley of Slades Beck). After White Stones, the path ascends mostly on the R side of the ridge crest to Carl Side. Descend to Carlside Tarn, on a narrow hause. From here, either ascend northeastwards with a path to the south cairn on Skiddaw, or ascend north-north-eastwards on a path which leads to the summit ridge of Skiddaw near the middle summit, height 928 m, south of the highest cairn, 931 m.

Jenkin Hill

Little Man

Plate 133 **Route 68** is a long plod

Robinson   Hindscarth   Dale Head

Cat Bells

Jaws of Borrowdale

Derwentwater

Latrigg

Keswick

Path from Keswick

To Jenkin Hill

A full western prospect from **Route 68** NB—Many trees on Latrigg have been felled

Blencathra

Lakeland visitors usually walk up from Keswick to Castlerigg Stone Circle, which stands in a bleak situation (GR 291236) at just over 210 m above sea level. Oval in shape, it has a diameter of about 30 m and commands some fine views of the surrounding fells. Most imposing of these is Blencathra, with its ridges rising to the summit, Hallsfell Top. The view in the reverse direction from this coign of vantage reveals the Grasmoor fells, from Causey Pike to Grisdale Pike.

The various routes to the summit of Blencathra, known also as Saddleback, are as follows:

Route 70. Scales and Sharp Edge. There are two approaches to Sharp Edge from Scales: The first is circuitous, but at an easy gradient; the second is direct and very steep, but reveals the most spectacular aspect of the lateral southern spurs of Blencathra.

For the former route, the key is the well-trodden path running parallel to, but well above, the upper River Glenderamackin. It may be reached from Scales by one of two variations: (a) From the minor road at GR 349272, take the path which rises through Mousthwaite Comb and bears R to emerge on a hause overlooking the river. At this point turn sharp L and follow the direct and almost level path for Scales Beck. (b) From Scales Green, GR 340268, take the path north to the open fell. Thence a path on R ascends the southern flanks of Scales Fell then swings round its eastern slopes, at the edge of Mousthwaite Comb, to join variation (a) some distance from the hause. On reaching Scales Beck, by variation (a) or (b), cross it and ascend the path beside Scales Beck to Scales Tarn.

For the latter route, reach the open fell from Scales Green, GR 340268. Climb the steep southern slopes of Scales Fell, keeping well to L to overlook the lower Doddick Fell. Diverge to R near the top, when Scales Tarn will be seen below. Descend to its outflow, Scales Beck.

After reaching the foot of Scales Tarn, by one of the two approaches described above, bear up the path on the grassy slopes to attain the eastern terminus of Sharp Edge. The crest of this narrow ridge may be traversed by those with a steady head and good balance, but it is easier and safer to keep to R just below it until the *mauvais pas* is reached. This is a short hiatus in the ridge and to cross it requires courage and a bold step or two to gain the path which continues to the foot of the inclined slabs that form the steep escarpment of Foule Crag. Great care is necessary here, especially after rain when the slabs are wet and slippery, but a little chimney on R facilitates progress. On gaining the summit plateau, which is expansive and forms the conspicuous 'saddle' of Saddleback, bear to L (south) for Hallsfell Top.

The panorama from Blencathra is one of the most extensive and unobstructed in Lakeland. The whole range of High Street is laid bare to the south-east and ends with the shapely cone of Ill Bell. Helvellyn is seen end-on to the south and is thus uninteresting, but the vista up St John's in the Vale with Thirlmere beyond is a delight and more than compensates for its tameness. The lower half of Derwentwater is revealed in the south-west and to R of Walla Crag, while the whole skyline beyond is resplendent with the familiar peaks of Scafell Pike and Great Gable, together with the Dale Head and Grasmoor fells. Skiddaw appears as a shapeless mass to the west and the vast solitudes of the Uldale and Caldbeck Fells stretch away into the dim distance to the north.

Route 71. Threlkeld and Hall's Fell. From Threlkeld a section of old road runs north-east to Gategill, which is situated below Hall's Fell. Pass the farm on R and keep the stream, Gate Gill, on R until the open fell is gained. Cross the stream and strike up the spur, which is at first grassy, then thickly covered with heather, until finally a splendid rock arête leads up to the summit of the mountain.

Plate 135 Blencathra from Castlerigg Stone Circle

Castlerigg Stone Circle

Plate 137 Blencathra from the east—**Route 70** and variations

Foule Crag

Sharp Edge

Plate 139 **Route 71** involves a continuous steepness

Route 72. Keswick and Blease Fell. From Briar Rigg, Keswick, take the minor road east for Windebrowe, or reach the road by crossing Calvert's Bridge, which spans the River Greta. Follow the road which threads the lovely Brundholme Wood fringing the northern banks of the river. Descend the road almost to Brundholme. (An alternative approach to Brundholme is by way of the path along the former railway line, with many crossings of the river). Cross Glenderaterra Beck by footbridge and ascend the path to Derwentfolds. From here a short section of road east leads to the start of the path to Blencathra Centre. Ascend the slopes of Blease Fell, north-eastwards, on a path which initially takes a wide zigzag. The top of Blease Fell is attained at Knowe Crags. Walk along the ridge which sweeps round high above the fine southern spurs of the mountain until Hallsfell Top is reached. This route is much finer in the reverse direction when the western panorama is spread out at one's feet during the whole of the descent.

Plate 140 **Route 72** is the best descent for views

Blencathra summit

Doddick Fell

Hall's Fell

Plate 141. The Blencathra ridges in Alpine conditions

← To Halls Fell Top

Foule Crag

Plate 142 **Route 70** crosses Sharp Edge

Plate 148. Route 70.—Fell walkers crossing Sharp Edge in dense mist

The Helvellyn group

Helvellyn	950 metres	3117 feet
Lower Man	925 metres	3035 feet
Nethermost Pike	891 metres	2923 feet
Catstye Cam	890 metres	2920 feet
Raise	883 metres	2897 feet
White Side	863 metres	2831 feet
Dollywaggon Pike	858 metres	2815 feet

OS Map: Landranger 90 Penrith, Keswick & Ambleside
Outdoor Leisure 5 North Eastern Area

Helvellyn
Route 73. Patterdale and Swirral Edge. From Patterdale take
the narrow road on L, short of Grisedale Bridge. Note that there
is no parking allowed on this road in Grisedale. There is
limited parking available in Patterdale, and so an alternative is
to leave transport in the adjoining village of Glenridding.
Route 73 can be joined in Grisedale by way of Lanty's Tarn
from Glenridding. An alternative approach to Route 73 from
Glenridding is detailed later in this route description.

The road from near Grisedale Bridge skirts the grounds of
Patterdale Hall, and in about half a mile rises into lower
Grisedale, where the route ahead towards 'Hole-in-the-Wall' is
revealed. Take the track rising ahead to the fellside at Brow-
nend Plantation. The path from Glenridding via Lanty's Tarn
arrives here. Ascend the path westwards on the flanks of
Birkhouse Moor. The route is now unmistakable, and when the
path bifurcates, at height about 490 m, take the right or upper
branch, because it will mitigate the steepness of the final rise
to 'Hole-in-the-Wall'. The views down into Grisedale are very
fine and improve as height is gained, while the retrospect of

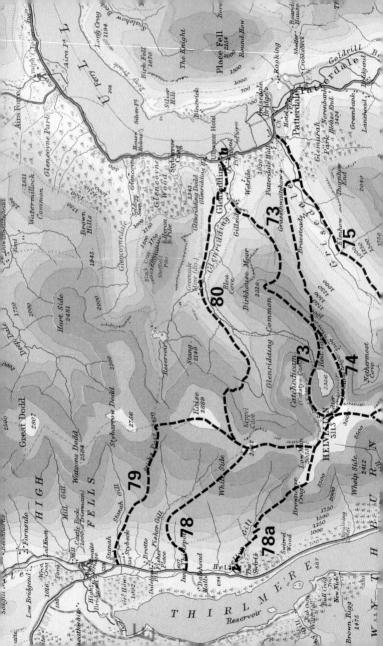

Map 8
Helvellyn
Routes 73 to 80

Patterdale and the head of Ullswater is also worthy of obser-
vation from time to time.

Route 73 may be joined at 'Hole-in-the-Wall' by the following
approach from Glenridding. From Rattlebeck Bridge, take the
track then path rising south-west to the open fell. Ascend the
path south-westwards in Little Cove, near Mires Beck. From
near the long wall descending the fellside in a west/east
direction, the path rises on to the crest of Birkhouse Moor. It
has been diverted away from the wall to control erosion. On
reaching the higher ground, the path bears L, alongside the
wall, to reach 'Hole-in-the-Wall'.

The majestic eastern front of Helvellyn is disclosed from near
'Hole-in-the-Wall', together with a foreshortened aspect of
Striding Edge on L, and of Catstye Cam and Swirral Edge on R.

From 'Hole-in-the-Wall' take the path westwards until Red
Tarn is seen at the foot of the Helvellyn precipices. Then bear
to R over the boggy ground past its outflow and keep to the
path which rises obliquely below Catstye Cam to attain the
ridge at a saddle. A short detour may be made to the summit
of Catstye Cam. Ascend the easy crags on the crest of Swirral
Edge ridge, which ultimately peters out on the vast summit
plateau, and then bear to L along the edge of the precipices for
the top of Helvellyn.

The panorama from Helvellyn is one of the most famous in
Lakeland and especially notable for its combination of lake and
fell. To the north the Dodds rise one after the other in an almost
direct line with Blencathra, whose lateral spurs are visible at
this great distance. Skiddaw stands nobly on their L. Bassenthwaite Lake can be seen from the ground near the Ordnance
Survey pillar. To the south the vast plateau sinks gently beyond
the cross-shaped summit shelter, and rises again to Dollywaggon Pike, on the other side of which appear the glimmering
waters of Windermere and Esthwaite Water. Fairfield rises on
L and is connected with St Sunday Crag by a high undulating
ridge where Cofa Pike and Deepdale Hause are well seen. To

Plate 144 **Routes 73** and **74** are steep on the approach to Hole-in-the-Wall

Dollywaggon Pike

Striding Edge

Hole-in-the-wall

Lower Track

the east the long ridge of High Street sweeps across the horizon, and on a clear day the dim outline of the Pennines may be perceived beyond. In the middle distance the lower and central sections of Ullswater are visible between Sheffield Pike and the end of Birkhouse Moor, while Red Tarn lies in the great hollow immediately below. To the west, however, the vista is more arresting, for it discloses the dominance of Scafell Pike over the galaxy of familiar peaks clustered together in the centre of Lakeland. Coniston Water gleams in the south with the bulky Coniston Fells on its R, from which Grey Friar seems to stand aloof. The serrated skyline then rises from Wrynose Pass over Crinkle Crags and Bowfell to Scafell Pike, to fall again at Great End to Lingmell and Glaramara before rising sharply to the conspicuous bald top of Great Gable. Pillar is the next clearly defined summit, followed by the High Stile range and finally by the Grasmoor hills, where Grisedale Pike appears as a graceful sentinel on the north-western horizon. The foreground of this vast prospect is confused and of comparatively little interest, Ullscarf occupying the major position in a line with Scafell Pike. Thirlmere is not seen from Helvellyn summit.

Route 74. Patterdale and Striding Edge. This is one of the most spectacular mountain walks in Lakeland but it can be dangerous in severe winter conditions. Reach 'Hole-in-the-Wall' from Patterdale, or from Glenridding, as described under Route 73. Ascend the path on L towards Striding Edge. A better variation is to keep to the edge of the crags on L and to adhere to the ridge crest all the way to High Spying How at the eastern end of Striding Edge. Then scramble along the Edge proper with care. The final descent to a saddle, by way of a rock step, needs special care. Scramble up the rocky, eroded slopes ahead, and on emerging on the skyline turn to R past the Gough Memorial, and walk up to the summit of Helvellyn. The views down on either side of Striding Edge are especially fine and justly famous for their impressiveness.

Catstye Cam

Swirral Edge

Helvellyn

Gough Memorial

Plate 145 **Route 73** is stony near the top

Hole-in-the-Wall

High Spying How

Striding Edge

Saddle

Plate 146. **Route 74**—The approach to Striding Edge is easy

Swirral Edge

Red Tarn

Nethermost Cove

Plate 147 Crossing Striding Edge by **Route 74**

Grisedale

Track

Hole-in-the-Wall

Step

Red
Tarn

Route 75. Grisedale and Dollywaggon Pike. Leave Patterdale by Route 73, and keep straight on along the road, which gives access to the deeper recesses of Grisedale. The route is unmistakable, first by cart track to Elmhow, then as a track to the bridge spanning the beck just beyond its junction with the stream coming down from Ruthwaite Cove.

Here the wild prospect is magnificent with the long escarpments of Dollywaggon Pike and Nethermost Pike descending steeply to the west, and shut in on L by the precipitous slopes of St Sunday Crag, and on R by Striding Edge.

Follow the path to Ruthwaite Lodge, and then bear to L and ascend the increasingly steep and rough path. A large cairn at GR 352123, close to the Brothers' Parting Stone, marks the bifurcation of the path on the fellside near the foot of Grisedale Tarn. Take the R branch and ascend the long zigzags to the main ridge, and then leave the path for the cairn of Dollywaggon Pike on R. Now advance along the edge of the cliffs, including the top of Nethermost Pike, all the way to the summit of the reigning peak, seen ahead. The views to the east and west are superb, and include a striking vista down the full length of Grisedale where Place Fell rises at the head of Ullswater far below.

Route 76. Grasmere and Grisedale Tarn. From the A591 road at GR 336092, just north of Mill Bridge, take the cart road to the open fell, where a conspicuous grassy tongue, Great Tongue, is seen ahead. Keep to the well-marked path which ascends the fell near Tongue Gill (east of Great Tongue), until Grisedale Hause is reached. From here Grisedale Tarn is disclosed some distance below. Follow the path on its eastern side and cross the boggy ground near its foot to the large cairn at GR 352123, already mentioned in Route 75, which follow to the summit of the mountain.

Route 77. From Wythburn. This route leaves the road near Wythburn church (GR 324136). Take the path eastwards through the trees then with zigzags, until Comb Gill is almost reached, on the open fell. The route then bends to R below Comb Crag and thereafter sweeps round to L to join Route 75, at the hause of Swallow Scarth, for the summit of the mountain.

Route 78. Thirlspot and White Side. From near the King's Head, Thirlspot, take the path which goes east, across the aqueduct, then ascends north-east to beyond a wall corner. Ascend the path north-east and swing round to R on approaching Fisherplace Gill. The path then goes south-eastwards, with the stream on L, and Brown Crag on R, to height about 660 m on the flank of White Side. Ascend the steep slopes of this eminence, following path traces and a few cairns, until the main ridge is attained at its summit, at Whiteside Bank. Then bear to R, southwards, to follow the ridge path over Lower Man for the summit of Helvellyn.

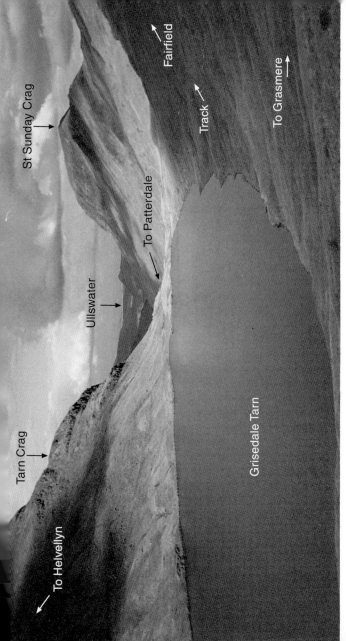

Plate 149 **Routes 75, 76 and 84** converge at the tarn outflow

Catstye Cam

Striding Edge

Helvellyn

Nethermost Pike

Dollywagon Pike

Tarn Crag

Fairfield

To Grisedale Tarn

Routes 75 and 76 are well seen from Fairfield

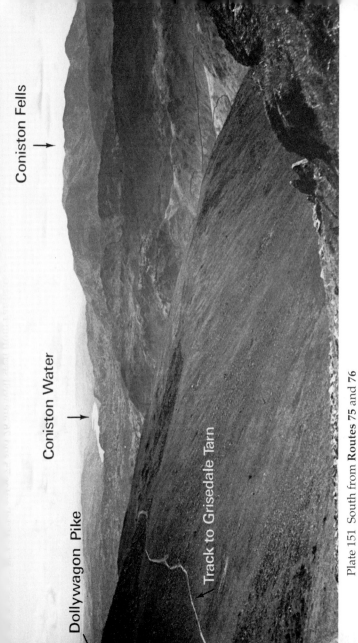

Coniston Fells

Coniston Water

Dollywagon Pike

Track to Grisedale Tarn

Plate 151 South from **Routes 75** and **76**

Crinkle Crags • Bowfell • Esk Pike • Scafell Pike • Great End • Glaramara • Great Gable • Red Pike (Wasdale) • Pillar • High Crag • Haystacks • High Stile • Red Pike

Lingmell • Ullscarf • Wyth Burn • Thirlmere • To Helvellyn • To Grisedale Tarn

Looking south-west from Routes 75 and 76

Esthwaite Water

Windermere

Great Rigg

Fairfield

Deepdale Hause

Dollywaggon Pike

Track to
Grisedale Tarn
and Wythburn

Helvellyn
Shelter

Plate 153 South from Helvellyn summit

Route 78a. The Swirls and Browncove Crags. An alternative approach from Thirlspot starts at The Swirls car-park at GR 316166. Take the path south-east. After crossing Helvellyn Gill twice, the path ascends in a series of zigzags, before rising towards the eroded slopes leading on to Browncove Crags. Here there is a reconstructed pathway. The route then passes Lower Man to its south, or a short detour leads on to its small summit. Helvellyn summit is reached by the ridge path.

Route 79. Sticks Pass and Raise. This is the second highest main pass in the Lake District and involves a long and circuitous route to Helvellyn. It would therefore seldom be chosen in preference to one of the more direct ascents and is only included for completeness. Leave the Keswick–Grasmere road at its junction with the road going north through St John's in the Vale. Walk up the road east to the farmstead of Stanah, and cross the gill at the end of the field behind it. Ascend the zigzag path as far as a sheepfold at height about 490 m. Then leave the stream on L and ascend the shoulder of Stybarrow Dodd until well above Sticks Gill. On attaining the top of the pass, which is now near at hand, turn to R along the broad crest of the main ridge and walk over Raise, White Side, and Lower Man to reach the summit of Helvellyn.

Route 80. Glenridding and Keppel Cove. From Glenridding car-park, walk up the road westwards to the disused Greenside Mine. Here pick up the grassy path that skirts the slopes, high above the stream on L, and which heads for the ruined dam in Keppel Cove. Some distance short of the dam, at GR 352166, opposite the riven northern slopes of Catstye Cam, bear R on the zigzag path rising to the rim of the cove. Thence follow the lofty skyline encircling both Keppel and Brown Coves to join Route 79, at White Side, for the summit of Helvellyn.

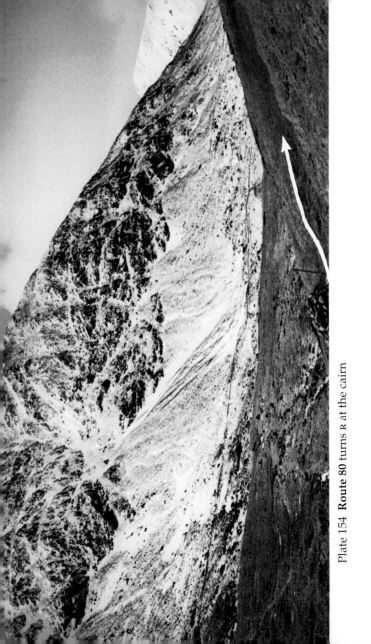

Plate 154 **Route 80 turns R at the cairn**

Top of Swirral Edge

Lower Man

The Fairfield group

Fairfield	873 metres	2864 feet
St Sunday Crag	841 metres	2759 feet
Hart Crag	822 metres	2697 feet
Dove Crag	792 metres	2598 feet
Red Screes	776 metres	2546 feet
Great Rigg	766 metres	2513 feet
High Pike	656 metres	2152 feet
Kirkstone Pass	*455 metres*	*1492 feet*

OS Map: Landranger 90 Penrith, Keswick & Ambleside
Outdoor Leisure 5 North Eastern Area
Outdoor Leisure 7 South Eastern Area

Fairfield
Route 81. Ambleside and High Pike. Leave the town by the Kirkstone Pass road and turn L at Nook Lane. This leads to the farmstead of Nook End. On the other side of the farm cross Scandale Beck at Low Sweden Bridge. Thereafter follow the track northwards with Low Pike ahead as the first eminence to be scaled. As height is gained there are beautiful views of the Rothay valley and Rydal on L, while low down on R the track for Patterdale is seen rising to Scandale Pass. The retrospect of Windermere also is delightful with its surface rippling away into the dim distance in the south. Keep to the crest of the ridge for High Pike, and note the two rocky knobs of Little Hart Crag above the pass on R. Continue ahead, alongside the old wall, until the cairn on Dove Crag is attained; then bear to L for Hart Crag. There are splendid prospects to R; first down Dovedale towards Brothers Water, and then down Deepdale to Patterdale, backed by Place Fell. Bear to L again after traversing Hart Crag and observe the fine precipitous bastion of Green-

Map 9
Fairfield
Routes 81 to 89

how End dropping down on R. Then make for the flat top of Fairfield, which is crowned by many cairns that can be very confusing in mist.

The panorama from Fairfield to east and west is not dissimilar to that from Helvellyn, but this mountain blocks much of the northern prospect and at the same time admirably reveals the topography of its grand subsidiary ridges. The view from the edge of the precipices enclosing the combe on the northeast is striking and will be a surprise to newcomers. It discloses the best aspect of Cofa Pike on L, beyond which the ground falls steeply to Deepdale Hause, to rise again gracefully to the summit of St Sunday Crag. The vista to the south is disappointing because the long escarpment of Great Rigg cuts out all of the valleys immediately below it. The distant view of Windermere, Esthwaite Water and Coniston Water is, however, a delight and especially on a clear day when the sunlight is reflected by them no less than by the great expanse of Morecambe Bay in the background.

Route 82. Rydal and Nab Scar. Note that there is no car-parking in Rydal village. A suitable place to park for this route is Pelter Bridge car-park, across the River Rothay at GR 365059.

Leave the village by ascending the steep road between the church and Rydal Mount on L and Rydal Hall on R. Ascend the steep path north-westwards, between two walls, for the open fell. Continue the ascent on the zigzag path until Nab Scar is attained. Linger to rest near where the path turns north, and admire the magnificent prospect to the south. The most striking features are Rydal Water and Grasmere over 300 m (1000 ft) below, together with the superlative vista down the Rothay valley to Windermere. Heron Pike rising to the north is the next objective, and its ascent still further widens the extensive retrospect. Thereafter the route is unmistakable, first along the crest of the ridge to Great Rigg and eventually to Fairfield summit.

Plate 156 **Route 81** as seen from Windermere

Route 83. Grasmere and Stone Arthur. Take the road beside the Swan Hotel, GR 340082, and in a short distance turn to R on a tarmac road near Greenhead Gill to the open fell. Turn to L and ascend the path between walls northwards then north-east then east. Then ascend the steep slopes of Stone Arthur on L (north). On reaching its rocky top, keep to the crest of the ridge for Great Rigg, and then follow Route 82 for the summit of Fairfield.

Route 84. Grasmere and Grisedale Tarn. Follow Route 76 until the tarn is revealed below and then ascend the rough slopes on R, beside a stone wall, which lead to the summit of the mountain.

Route 85. Patterdale and St Sunday Crag. Follow Route 73 for a short distance and turn in at a gate on L, at GR 387158, where a path goes across the field. Pick up the path south-south-west which rises between trees, and eventually reaches the wall on the brow of Thornhow End. The path continues in a south-westerly direction, obliquely across the flank of Birks to a hause at GR 376141, above Blind Cove.

Then advance over the broad grassy crest of the ridge towards St Sunday Crag, which rises to the south-west, keeping to the edge of the slopes high above Grisedale. The views to R of the precipitous eastern cliffs of the Helvellyn range are superb. From St Sunday Crag summit, the craggy combes of Fairfield, below Route 81, are well seen. The most delectable vista from the mountain is, however, seen in retrospect from the ground north of the summit during the ascent of this Route 85, since it reveals the head of Ullswater far below, together with the first graceful bend in the lake. The ridge narrows in the descent to Deepdale Hause and discloses a grand prospect of the wild combe at the head of Deepdale already referred to in Route 81. Cofa Pike rises ahead as a sharp point on the Fairfield ridge; scramble up the stony ridge, noting the bird's-eye view of Grisedale Tarn far below on R, and then make a short ascent south to set foot on the summit of the reigning peak.

Grisedale

Ullswater

Patterdale

Plate 157 **Route 85**

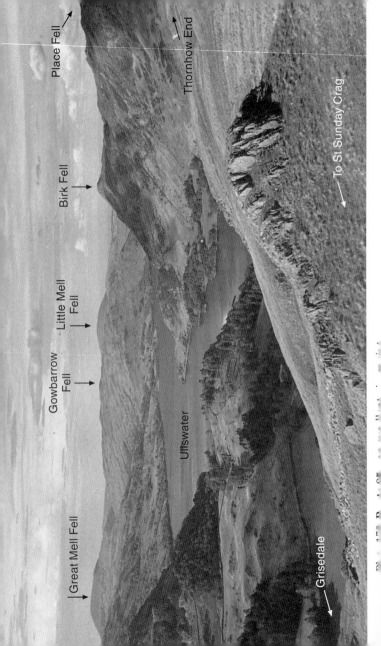

Place Fell

Thornhow End

Birk Fell

Little Mell Fell

Gowbarrow Fell

Great Mell Fell

Ullswater

Grisedale

To St Sunday Crag

Fairfield

Cofa Pike

Froswick   Ill Bell

Deepdale Hause

To St Sunday Crag

Tarn Crag

To Grisedale
Tarn

Grisedale

Plate 159 **Route 85**

Route 86. Patterdale and Deepdale. Leave the village by the Kirkstone Pass road, and diverge to R along a road west from Deepdale Bridge, at Bridgend GR 399144. This threads the lower reaches of the wide green strath of Deepdale, and passes cottages at Lane Head, and Deepdale Hall, before terminating at Wall End. Continue along the grassy track on the north side of the stream with Greenhow End rising ahead. On approaching this rocky bastion, cross the main stream and follow its southern tributary which has its source in Link Cove below Hart Crag. Ascend the steep slopes near a gully on L, south-eastwards, to reach the ridge north-east of Hart Crag top, at GR 374114. Ascend the ridge south-west to Hart Crag summit. Then follow the ridge, as Route 81, for Fairfield summit.

Hart Crag   Link Hause   Scrubby Crag   Greenhow End   Fairfield   Cofa Pike   Deepdale Hause

Dove Crag   Hart Crag

The Stangs

Hartsop Hall

Plate 162 **Route 87**—Dovedale. The crag has many rock climbs

Route 87. Patterdale and Dovedale. Leave the village by the Kirkstone Pass road, and on approaching Brothers Water take the track on R, at Cow Bridge, which passes beneath the trees fringing the shore of the lake. Go as far as the first barn beyond Hartsop Hall and then bear R up the grassy cart track to some old mine workings. Now enter the woods and keep on the path with a wall on L until you reach the cross wall, whence follow the well-marked path that swings across the steep slopes of Hartsop above How. Keep the beck on L until you enter the boulder-strewn Houndshope Cove, with Dove Crag towering overhead. On reaching it bear R and scramble up the rough slopes of the combe, and on attaining the crest of the ridge pick up Route 81 for Fairfield.

A more romantic approach follows the path south-west from Hartsop Hall to Dovedale Beck. Thence it continues as a path on the south side of the beck, passing close to the waterfalls. The route described above can be joined by crossing the beck at height about 340 m, north of Stangs.

Note – An attractive alternative to Routes 86 and 87 is the easy traverse of Hartsop above How, an undulating grassy ridge separating the two dales. It has the merit of disclosing a bird's-eye view of each, together with Dove Crag on L, and Link Cove on R. The latter is one of the wildest in this part of Lakeland and is enclosed by the shattered front of Hart Crag, the cliffs of Scrubby Crag, and the terminal precipices of Greenhow End.

The ridge of Hartsop above How is gained by a path starting from the road at GR 402141, south-east of Deepdale Bridge.

Route 88. Brothers Water, Caiston Glen and Scandale Pass.
Reach Hartsop Hall from either Cow Bridge as described under
Route 87, or via the track west from Brotherswater Inn. Take
the path southwards, west of Kirkstone Beck, then ascend the
path beside Caiston Beck. Follow this stream in Caiston Glen
to Scandale Pass. Turn to R and ascend the flank of Little Hart
Crag. A short detour can be made to its twin tops. Breast the
slopes ahead, across Bakestones Moss, to the cairn above Dove
Crag, and there join Route 81 for Fairfield.

Route 89. Kirkstone Pass and Red Screes. This craggy hill
rises to the north-west of the Kirkstone Pass Inn. There is a
path with a few variations possible, ascending its steep flanks
to the summit. This commands a superlative prospect of
Windermere, a part only of its upper reaches being hidden by
the ridge of Wansfell. In addition to the bird's-eye view of the
Kirkstone Pass far below, it reveals much of the western
panorama as seen from Helvellyn, and a fine view of the High
Street range.

   The route for Fairfield is to the north-west, where a wall may
be picked up which falls to Scandale Pass. Here Route 88 is
joined and traversed to the reigning peak.

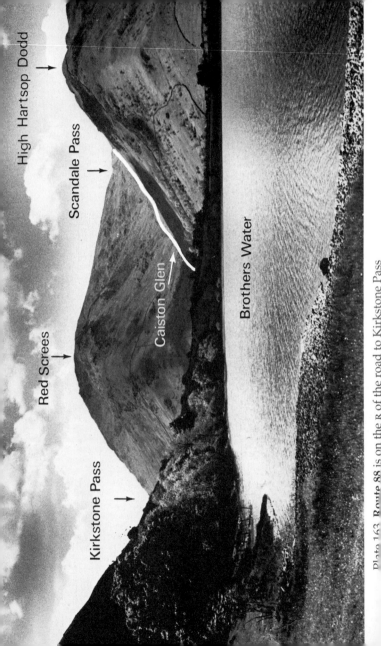

High Hartsop Dodd

Scandale Pass

Red Screes

Kirkstone Pass

Caiston Glen

Brothers Water

Plate 163. Route 88 is on the R of the road to Kirkstone Pass

Plate 164 **Routes 81, 86 and 87** from St. Sunday Crag

Dove Crag

Hart Crag

Scandale Pass

Dovedale

Greenhow End

Deepdale

High Street, North

High Street	828 metres	2716 feet
High Raise	802 metres	2631 feet
Rampsgill Head	792 metres	2598 feet
Thornthwaite Crag	784 metres	2572 feet
Kidsty Pike	c780 metres	2559 feet
Mardale Ill Bell	760 metres	2493 feet
Wether Hill	c673 metres	2208 feet

OS Map: Landranger 90 Penrith, Keswick & Ambleside
Outdoor Leisure 5 North Eastern Area
Outdoor Leisure 7 South Eastern Area

High Street, North

Route 90. Patterdale and Pasture Beck. Leave the village by the Kirkstone Pass road and take the branch road for Hartsop. Pass through the village and park your car in a large space beyond the last cottage. Take the track which crosses the stream south. Keep the wall then stream on L, as you approach Pasture Bottom, between Gray Crag on L, and Hartsop Dodd on R. Raven Crag is the conspicuous outcrop of rock high above the stream. Keep this on R and follow the path which threads Threshthwaite Cove and rises to the dip in the skyline ahead. Bear to L here and scale the loose shaly slopes of Thornthwaite Crag, which is crowned by a high slender cairn. This viewpoint is a revelation to the newcomer, for it opens up an extensive panorama to the south where Windermere glitters away into the dim distance backed by Morecambe Bay, and also discloses much of the topography of High Street to the north-east. Now drop down and advance across the boggy ground in this direction, picking up the stone wall which runs up to the summit of the mountain.

Threlkeld Crag → Threshthwaite Cove → Threshthwaite Crag →

Plate 165 **Route 90** follows Pasture Beck to the gap in the skyline

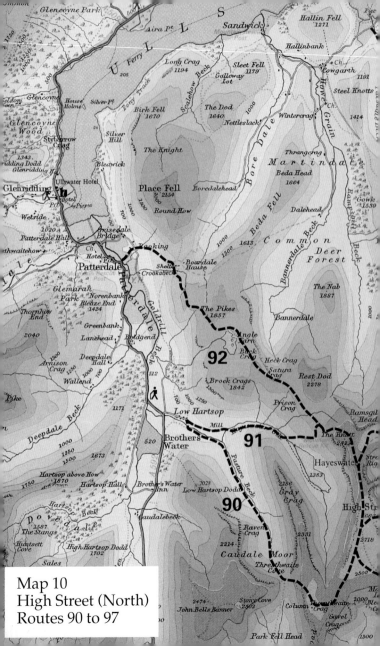

Map 10
High Street (North)
Routes 90 to 97

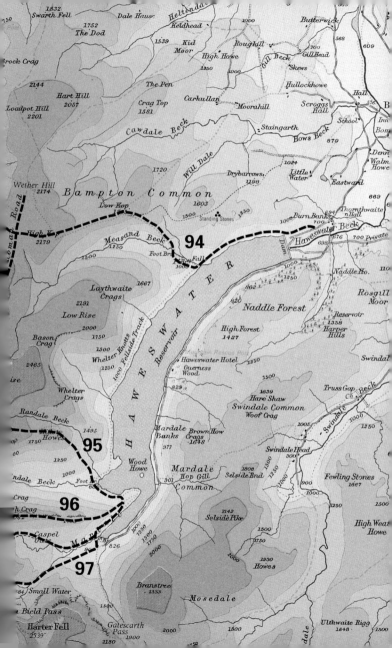

The panorama from High Street is interesting, but owing to the width of the plateau it is desirable to walk some distance from the cairn to see all but the western section of the arc. To the north the high ridge undulates as far as the eye can see with the conspicuous stone wall running along its many ups and downs and where traces of the Roman road may be perceived immediately on its left. Place Fell, The Knott and Kidsty Pike are prominent in the foreground, while Blencathra, Carrock Fell and Great Mell Fell rise on the distant horizon. To the south the view is largely obscured by Mardale Ill Bell and Harter Fell, Froswick and Ill Bell, and the ridge running up to Thornthwaite Crag, but the lower reaches of Windermere are visible. To the east Long Stile drops steeply to Caspel Gate, and its continuation, the ridge of Rough Crag, rises above the head of Haweswater, a glimpse of which is seen on L. The background is rather confused by the wild moorland of the Shap Fells, above which the Pennine skyline discloses Cross Fell on L and Ingleborough on R. The extensive prospect to the west is, however fascinating because it comprises the full length of the Fairfield and Helvellyn groups, dominated by Scafell and Scafell Pike. Taken as a whole, the most outstanding features are as follows from left to right. The Coniston Fells are prominent on L of Red Screes whose summit is seen beyond the stone-walled top of Caudale Moor. Crinkle Crags, Bowfell and the Scafells then rise above the dip of Scandale Pass with the bald top of Great Gable between Dove Crag and Hart Crag. Then comes the scarped front of Fairfield with a glimpse of High Stile and Red Pike on R above the Grisedale Hause gap. Thereafter the Helvellyn range sweeps across the horizon to Great Dodd, which is backed by the massive form of Skiddaw in the north-west.

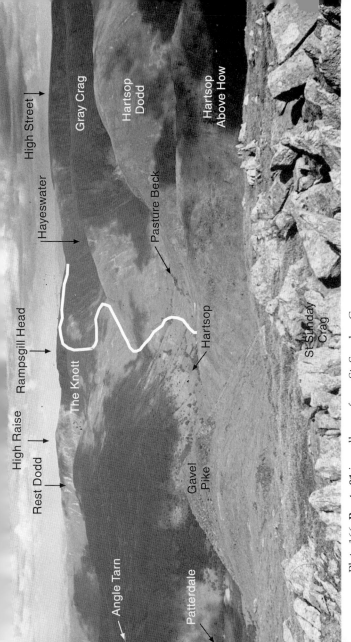

Plate 166 **Route 91** is well seen from St. Sunday Crag

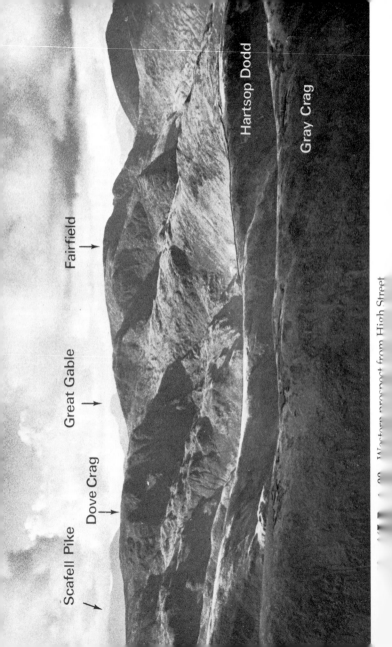

Scafell Pike Great Gable Fairfield

Dove Crag

Hartsop Dodd

Gray Crag

Western prospect from High Street

Route 91. Patterdale and Hayeswater. Follow Route 90 to Hartsop. Now walk along the road eastwards, and take the track which crosses Hayeswater Gill at GR 417129. The track rises to R and ends at the dam of Hayeswater. From the dam, or from a short distance short of it, walk to L towards The Knott, on a zigzag path passing round it to L, and so gain the path by the wall which runs from the Straits of Riggindale up to the reigning peak.

Route 92. Patterdale and Angle Tarn. Turn to L along the road which diverges, at GR 398158, from the highway in the village, and at Rooking ascend either of the two paths on R. These rise to Boredale (Boardale) Hause, which discloses a fine retrospect of the head of Ullswater. Take the path rising southwards, and pass round Angletarn Pikes on L, when Angle Tarn soon appears in a grassy hollow below. Bear to L and skirt its eastern shore, passing Buck Crag and Satura Crag for The Knott straight ahead. Hereabouts there are some fine vistas down the wide green strath of Bannerdale, and many walkers may choose to diverge to L to ascend Rest Dodd, which reveals an even better prospect of the two dales to the north. Then join Route 91, and walk up to the brow of The Knott where the path swings round behind it for High Street.

Plate 169 **Route 92**—Helvellyn from Angle Tarn—a popular resting place for fell walkers

Route 93. Howtown and Wether Hill. From near the Howtown Hotel take the road which gives access to Fusedale due south. Follow the track then path southwards with the beck first on L and then on R. After crossing Groove Gill, a tributary which comes down on L, make for the ruined hut at GR 447169. Take the path heading south-eastwards on the flank of Wether Hill. The view to R into the deep recesses of Ramps Gill is very fine, with the conspicuous spur known as The Nab on R. On attaining the ridge, near a wall, a short detour north-east takes you to Wether Hill. Follow the line of the Roman road along the ridge, over High Raise. Diverge to L for the cairn on Kidsty Pike, which reveals perhaps the most comprehensive aspect of High Street. Then skirt Rampsgill Head and drop down to the Straits of Riggindale to pick up Route 92 for the summit.

Route 94. Mardale and Measand Beck. From the minor road at GR 508161, at Burnbanks, walk along the track westwards, which takes a zigzag to reach the fell above the trees. Continue along the path westwards above Haweswater. Measand Beck is about a mile along this path; cross it and ascend the south bank, recrossing it again by a footbridge. Then walk up the fellside north to near a stream, then north-westwards, past an old quarry to Low Kop. Keep to the high ground westwards for High Kop, and Wether Hill. Here join Route 93 for High Street.

Route 95. Mardale and Kidsty Pike. From the road terminus at Mardale Head, pass through a gate, and turn to R to cross Mardale Beck. Turn to R again and keep to the path which passes above and behind The Rigg, the wooded spur jutting out into Haweswater. Drop down to Riggindale Beck, and keeping Randale Beck on R ascend the grassy slopes of Kidsty Howes. On attaining the high ground, bear to L high above the beck until Kidsty Pike appears ahead. Here join Route 93 for the summit of the reigning peak.

Plate 170 **Routes 91, 92 and 93,** looking north along the wall on High Street

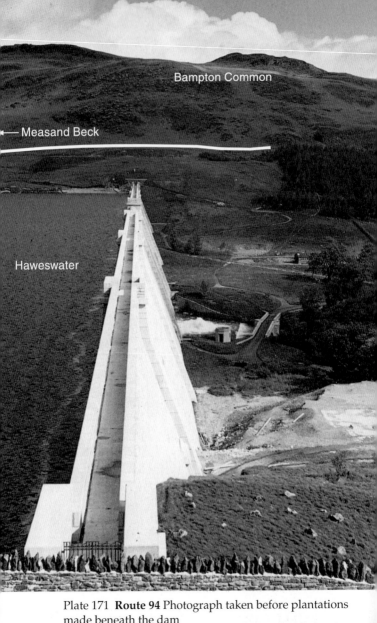

Bampton Common

← Measand Beck

Haweswater

Plate 171 **Route 94** Photograph taken before plantations made beneath the dam

High Street → | Short Stile → | Kidsty Pike →

Wood Howe

Haweswater

Plate 172 Looking across Haweswater to **Route 95**

Route 96. Mardale and Rough Crag. From the road terminus at Mardale Head, pass through a gate, and turn to R to cross Mardale Beck. Turn to L and keep to the beck. Then follow its tributary, Blea Water Beck, to the foot of Blea Water. Diverge to R for the hause of Caspel Gate, and afterwards ascend the craggy escarpment of Long Stile, which rises to the skyline immediately to the north of the summit of High Street.

Those wishing to traverse the full length of the Rough Crag ridge should follow Route 95 to above The Rigg, and then ascend the path on L, by a wall.

Route 97. Mardale and Nan Bield Pass. From the road terminus at Mardale Head, pass through a gate, and keep to the path which rises to the south-west, as far as Small Water, with Harter Fell on L, and Small Water Beck on R. Skirt the north-western side of the tarn and walk up the zigzag path to Nan Bield Pass, which is a prominent dip in the skyline. Then turn sharp to R up the slope of Mardale Ill Bell which discloses a fine view of the Ill Bell range, with the Kentmere valley and its reservoir down on L. Traverse the broad top, keeping to R, above Blea Water, and then follow the wall on the skyline which leads to the summit of High Street.

Plate 173 **Route 97**—Retrospect of Small Water from the track below Nan Bield

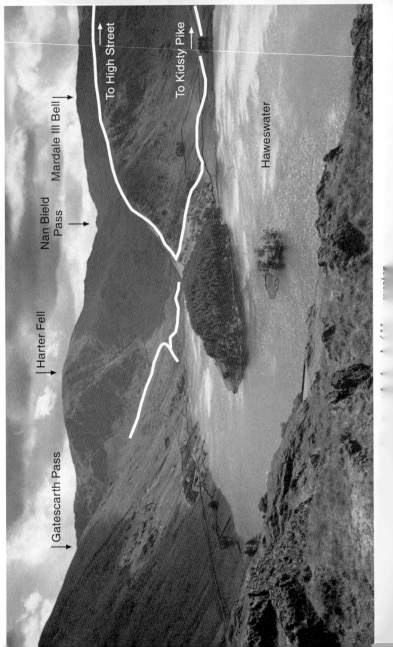

To High Street

To Kidsty Pike

Mardale Ill Bell

Nan Bield Pass

Harter Fell

Gatescarth Pass

Haweswater

Plate 175 **Route 96** keeps to the crest of Rough Crag and Caspel Gate

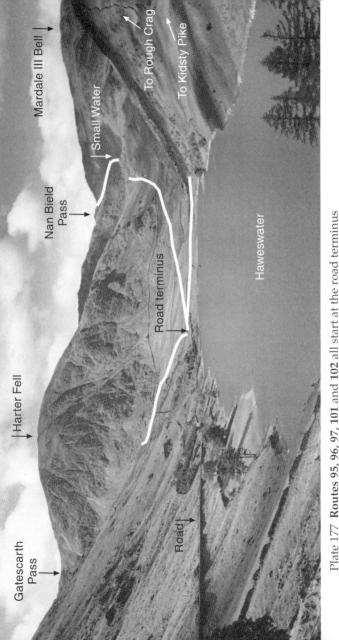

Plate 177 **Routes 95, 96, 97, 101** and **102** all start at the road terminus

High Street, South, and Harter Fell, Mardale

High Street	828 metres	2716 feet
Thornthwaite Crag	784 metres	2572 feet
Harter Fell	778 metres	2552 feet
Mardale Ill Bell	760 metres	2493 feet
Ill Bell	757 metres	2483 feet
Froswick	720 metres	2362 feet
Yoke	706 metres	2316 feet

OS Map: Landranger 90 Penrith, Keswick & Ambleside
Outdoor Leisure 5 North Eastern Area
Outdoor Leisure 7 South Eastern Area

High Street, South

Route 98. Kentmere and Nan Bield Pass. From Kentmere church, cross the River Kent at Low Bridge, and take the road heading for Green Quarter. From just short of Green Quarter, take the road (High Lane) heading northwards for Overend, GR 464057. An alternative is the track of Low Lane, passing close to the pretty falls of Force Jump. At Overend take the track on R and after another mile avoid the quarry track on R. Traverse the western flanks of Harter Fell with the Kentmere Reservoir low down on L and continue northwards to Nan Bield Pass, where turn L and pick up Route 97 for High Street.

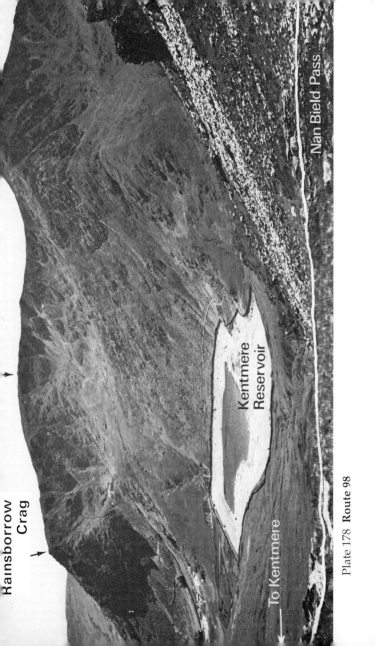

Rainsborrow
Crag

Nan Bield Pass

Kentmere
Reservoir

To Kentmere

Plate 178 Route 98

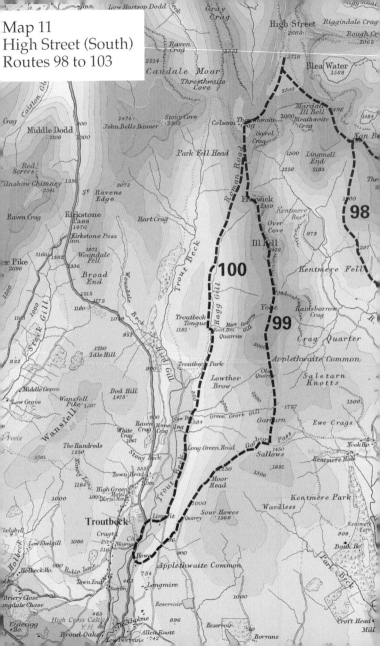

Map 11
High Street (South)
Routes 98 to 103

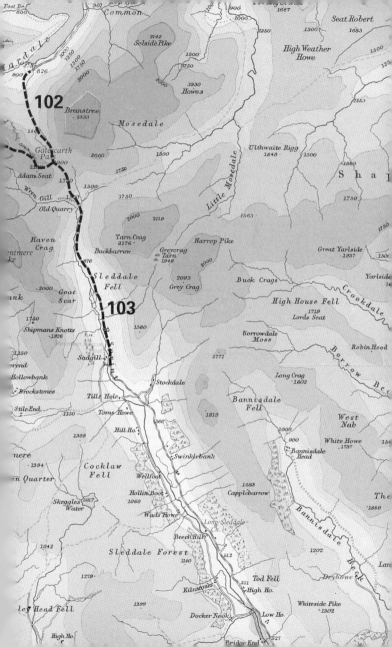

Route 99. Troutbeck and Ill Bell. Leave the village at the church, GR 413028, and cross Church Bridge. Take the track on L which continues as Garburn Road to Garburn Pass. From the pass, ascend the fell northwards, keeping to the L of a stone wall as far as the point where it bears sharp L. Cross the stile and pick up the path on the other side which rises gently to Yoke. Keep to the crest of the ridge for Ill Bell, whose summit is characterised by an array of cairns. The retrospect is splendid and discloses much the same view of Windermere as Thornthwaite Crag. Continue northwards by way of the peak of Froswick, to Thornthwaite Crag, beyond which pick up Route 90 for High Street.

Route 100. Troutbeck and Thornthwaite Crag. Leave the village at the church, GR 413028, and take the road into Limefitt Park. Here pick up the track for Long Green Head. Advance northwards at the foot of Lowther Brow and then keep straight on up the valley with The Tongue and Hagg Gill on L. Cross this stream near a disused quarry and keep it on R. Then commence the steep ascent of the Roman road which traverses the western flanks of Froswick. Walk up to Thornthwaite Crag, which towers ahead, and join Route 90 for High Street.

Plate 179 **Route 99** from Ill Bell

Thornthwaite Beacon

Ill Bell

Troutbeck

Harter Fell, Mardale

Route 101. From Nan Bield Pass. Ascend the path rising to the south-east from the top of the pass, reached by Route 97 from Mardale Head, or by Route 98 from Kentmere. Thence walk up the grassy slope to the summit cairn. Harter Fell is notable for two prospects, seen from viewpoints away from the summit cairn: the one of Mardale immediately below to the north with the long reaches of Haweswater glittering away into the distance, and flanked on the west by High Street at its best, and on the east by the featureless slopes about Guerness Wood; the other from The Knowe, which reveals the dalehead of Kentmere to advantage together with its shapely enclosing peaks on the west.

Route 102. Mardale and Gatescarth pass. From the road terminus at Mardale Head, pass through a gate, and take the track on L which winds upwards between Branstree on L and Harter Fell on R. On reaching the top of the pass, turn sharp to R and aim for Adam Seat. Here you turn R and keep to the path above the crags for the summit of Harter Fell.

Route 103. Long Sleddale and Gatescarth Pass. Leave the bridge, GR 483057, at Sadgill, the last farm in the dale, by the old quarry road which winds up the valley between two stone walls. Goat Scar and Raven Crag are the two rocky outcrops high up on L, while the shattered cliffs of Buckbarrow Crag frown down on R. The River Sprint provides plenty of water music until the disused quarry workings are reached. At Brownhowe Bottom avoid the path on R and leave Wrengill Quarry on L, to ascend the track over the grassy brow of the hill ahead and traverse some marshy ground before Gatescarth Pass is reached. Then bear to L and follow Route 102 for Harter Fell.

Plate 101—Haweswater from Harter Fell

Plate 182   **Route 101**—High Street and Blea Water from Harter Fell

Plate 102. Route 102. Tregharton Hamlets. Full range to the foreze from Adam Street

Plate 184 **Route 103** begins at Sadgill where the tarmac road ends

The Langdale Pikes

High Raise	762 metres	2500 feet
Harrison Stickle	736 metres	2415 feet
Ullscarf	726 metres	2382 feet
Thunacar Knott	723 metres	2372 feet
Pike o'Stickle	709 metres	2326 feet
Pavey Ark	c700 metres	2296 feet
Loft Crag	c670 metres	2198 feet
Silver How	395 metres	1296 feet

OS Map: Landranger 90 Penrith, Keswick & Ambleside
  Outdoor Leisure 4 North Western Area
  Outdoor Leisure 6 South Western Area
  Outdoor Leisure 7 South Eastern Area

The Langdale Pikes

Route 104. By Stickle Ghyll. From the drive near Sticklebarn and the New Dungeon Ghyll Hotel, at GR 295065, pass through the gateway, to the R of the white cottage. Either cross the footbridge over Stickle Ghyll, to take the path rising north-west, east of the ghyll, or take the path north-west, west of the ghyll. (The latter may be reached directly from the car-park south of Sticklebarn.) The routes join at a footbridge below (east of) Pike Howe. From this bridge, take the reconstructed path rising north-westwards, east of the ghyll. At GR 289072, on the approach to Tarn Crag, either cross the ghyll, care needed, and take the path north, or continue close to the ghyll, on its east side. Here, depending upon the route taken, some scrambling may be necessary. The dam at Stickle Tarn is a singularly wild viewpoint and reveals the great gullied cliffs of Pavey Ark on the other side of the tarn where it is connected with Harrison Stickle by a high ridge. Turn to L and walk due west over the

Plate 185 The western panorama from Windermere

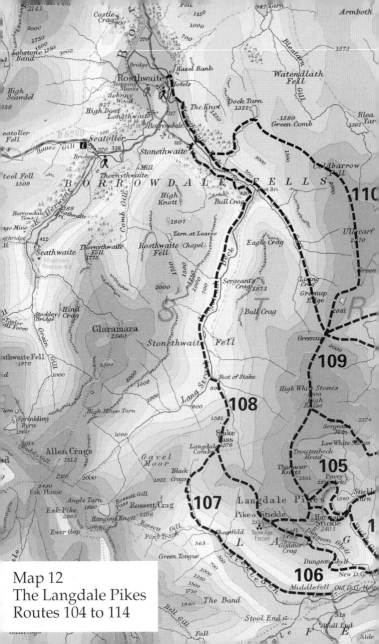

Map 12
The Langdale Pikes
Routes 104 to 114

grassy slopes at the base of Harrison Stickle, but skirt its crags on R and ascend the scree beside them to attain its flat summit.

The fine profile of these hills and their relationship to the adjacent Crinkle Crags/Bowfell group are well seen from the shores of Windermere in the vicinity of Low Wood. On entering the valley of Great Langdale beyond Chapel Stile, their majestic proportions are still more impressive and reveal at a glance the two principal routes to the summit.

The newcomer will find the panorama restricted by the engirdling hills. To the south-east the ground falls away to unfold the finest vista from the peak of Harrison Stickle. This comprises the wide green patterned strath of Great Langdale which leads the eye first to Elterwater and Windermere, then to R to Esthwaite Water and finally to the luminous surface of Blea Tarn, low down on R. The western prospect from Bowfell to the Gables is the best of the distant views, and its skyline also discloses Scafell Pike above Ore Gap, Great End above Esk Hause and the Gables above the long ridge rising to Glaramara.

Route 105. By Pavey Ark. Follow Route 104 to Stickle Tarn, where the topography of Pavey Ark reveals a prominent ledge known as Jack's Rake rising from R to L across its precipitous face, together with a great rift in the crags on R known as Easy Gully or East Gully. Jack's Rake is a scrambler's route, traversing fine rock scenery, and although generally easy-angled, has some steep sections. It is recommended to experienced scramblers only. Easy or East Gully is mainly a steep walk on grass and scree. It has one obstacle, involving a short rock scramble. The ascent of the latter is free from danger, and has the advantage of a close view of the crags of East Buttress and East Wall, which are popular with the rock climbing fraternity.

Skirt the shore of the tarn and ascend the bewildering array of boulders and scree to the mouth of the gully. (Here the start of Jack's Rake is seen on L.) While scaling the floor of the chasm of Easy Gully keep to L, as far as the gigantic boulders blocking

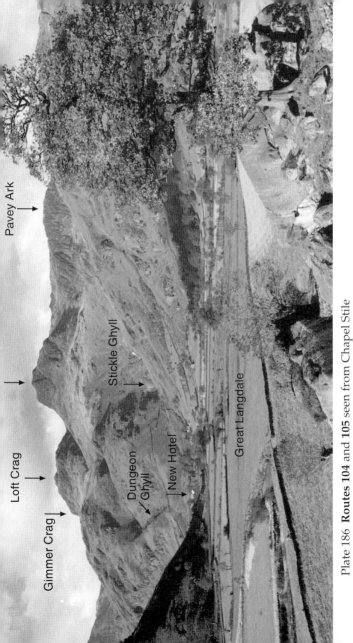

Plate 186 **Routes 104** and **105** seen from Chapel Stile

Harrison Stickle

Pavey Ark

Tarn Crag

Stickle Ghyll

New Dungeon Ghyll Hotel

Plate 188 **Route 104**—The former route on the ʟ of Stickle Ghyll. Take the path ʀ of the stream

Pavey Ark →

Easy Gully

Jacks Rake

Stickle Tarn

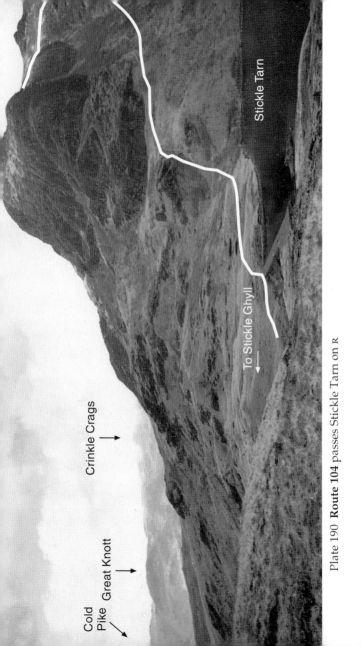

Plate 190 **Route 104** passes Stickle Tarn on R

its exit. Then move to R before making a short scramble move L (awkward) to attain the easy ground beyond the boulders. A grassy rake, known as North Rake, is reached, Follow this L, west, then make the short ascent southwards on to the rocky top of Pavey Ark. From here an interesting path goes south-west then south for Harrison Stickle.

Note – An alternative ascent to Pavey Ark involves following the full length of the North Rake, reached from near Bright Beck, to the north of Stickle Tarn.

Route 106. By Dungeon Ghyll and Pike o'Stickle. From Sticklebarn and the New Hotel, ascend the path westwards to where it crosses Dungeon Ghyll. Then ascend the path with the ghyll on R, and past the waterfall of Dungeon Ghyll Force. The path rises in a zigzag to above Raven Crag, a popular crag for rock climbers, easily reached from the Old Hotel by an erosion-control path. The path diverges to L below Thorn Crag, and swings round to reach the col R of Loft Crag. Now walk to L west, and ascend the path on to Loft Crag top, above Gimmer Crag. Then keep near to the edge of the cliffs on a path and afterwards ascend Pike o'Stickle, by a short easy scramble.

From Pike o'Stickle the view to the south-east is much finer than that from Harrison Stickle because it discloses the grand western façade of Gimmer Crag which frowns upon the walled strath of the dale some 600 m (2000 ft) below. It also reveals a bird's-eye view of Mickleden to the west which terminates with the fine rift of Rossett Gill. Descend in an easterly direction for Harrison Stickle, cross the stream and the inter-vening boggy ground, and walk up to the twin cairns on its flat summit ridge.

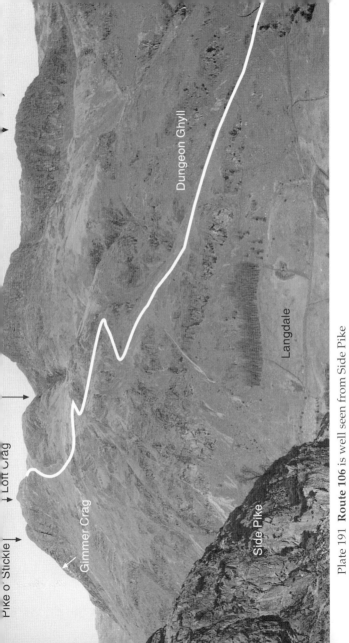

Pike o' Stickle | Loft Crag | Gimmer Crag | Pike o' Stickle

Dungeon Ghyll

Langdale

Side Pike

Plate 191 **Route 106** is well seen from Side Pike

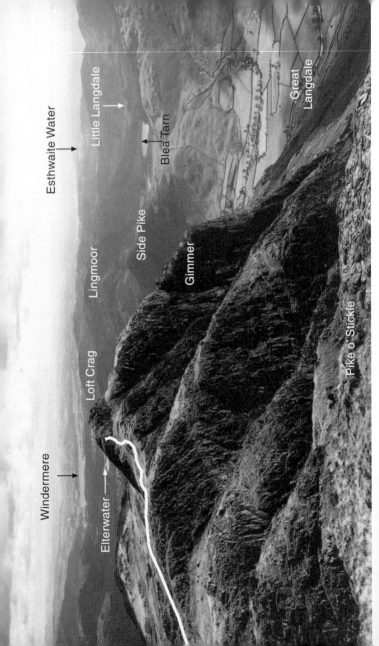

Windermere

Esthwaite Water

Little Langdale

Elterwater

Loft Crag

Lingmoor

Side Pike

Blea Tarn

Great
Langdale

Gimmer

Pike o' Stickle

Plate 193 **Route 106**—Final section seen from Pike o' Stickle

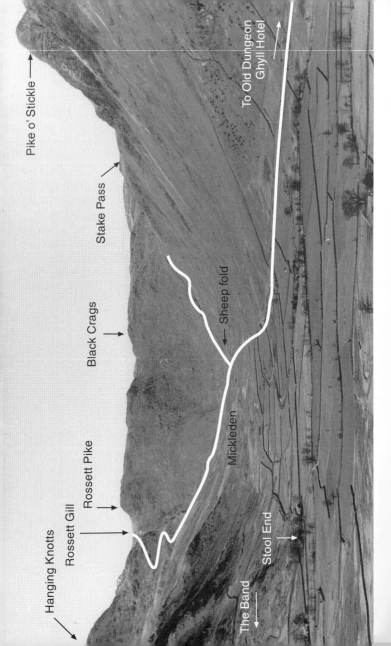

Pike o' Stickle →

Stake Pass

Black Crags →

Rossett Pike →

Hanging Knotts

Rossett Gill →

To Old Dungeon Ghyll Hotel

← Sheep fold

Mickleden

Stool End →

The Band

Route 107. Mickleden and Stake Pass. Take the track behind the Old Dungeon Ghyll Hotel. The prominent crag on the hillside above you to the north is Raven Crag, popular with rock climbers; Middlefell Buttress is on the left. The track runs alongside a stone wall for almost half the length of the Mickleden valley. Continue ahead over the green strath as far as the sheepfold, at GR 261073, situated near the end of the valley. Here the path forks, the left branch rising near Rossett Gill, and the right one zigzagging up the fellside to Langdale Combe and Stake Pass. Ascend the latter, beside Stake Gill, and on reaching the summit of the pass, turn to the R. Take a path across Martcrag Moor, then a path rising to the cone of Pike o'Stickle. A short scramble leads to its top. Descend in an easterly direction for Harrison Stickle, cross the stream and the intervening boggy ground, and walk up to the twin cairns on its flat summit ridge.

Route 108. Rosthwaite and Stake Pass. From Rosthwaite, or Stonethwaite, follow Route 31 to the footbridge at Stake Beck, at the foot of Stake Pass, in Langstrath. Ascend the winding path to the summit of the pass. Then follow Route 107, as described above, to Pike o'Stickle and Harrison Stickle.

Route 109. Greenup Gill and High Raise. Leave Rosthwaite by the bridge to Hazel Bank, and after crossing it turn to R and follow the track to Stonethwaite Beck. Access to this track from Stonethwaite is by Stonethwaite Bridge. Follow the track to near the confluence of Langstrath Beck and Greenup Gill. Follow the path rising near the latter, with the gill, Eagle Crag and Pounsey Crag on the R. As height is gained note the large number of moraines down on the R at the head of the valley. On approaching the rocky bastion of Lining Crag, you take the path ascending the steep slopes to its L (on its east side). On attaining the easier slopes above, keep to the south over some marshy ground for the wide hause of Greenup Edge. Then turn to the R, and follow the ridge over Low White Stones to High White Stones, at the summit of High Raise. This is a fine belvedere with a comprehensive panorama revealing a great number of familiar Lakeland peaks engirdling the whole horizon. The Langdale Pikes are to the south, Scafell Pike and Great Gable and their satellites appear in the west, and the two massive sentinels of Skiddaw and Blencathra rise on the northern skyline. The whole of the Helvellyn and Fairfield ranges close the prospect to the east. Proceed southwards over the vast undulating moorland solitudes, including Thunacar Knott, to attain the summit of Harrison Stickle.

Route 110. Dock Tarn and Ullscarf. From near Stonethwaite Bridge, ascend the steep path in the woods on the hillside on the L (north) of Willygrass Gill. The path continues to the foot of Dock Tarn. From here pick your way across the hollow of Green Combe to the rough slopes beyond. Now continue the ascent in a south-easterly direction for Coldbarrow Fell. Keep to the high ground, walk over Ullscarf, and descend to the hause of Greenup Edge. Thereafter follow Route 109 for the Langdale Pikes.

This interesting route has excellent views.

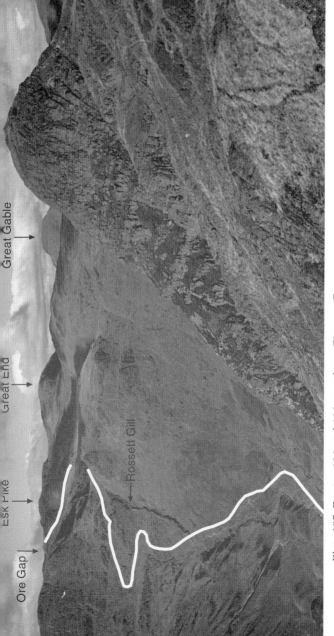

Plate 195 **Routes 106** and **116** seen from Gimmer Crag

Plate 197 **Route 109**—Western prospect from High White Stones

Honister Crag

High Stile

Grasmoor

Plate 198 An example of footpath improvement to be found on **Route 113**, below Easedale Tarn

Route 111. Wythburn and Greenup Edge. This ascent is unmistakable and follows the streams coming down the valley to the south-west of the head of Thirlmere. From Stockhow Bridge, take the path on the east side of Wyth Burn. An alternative start is the track from Steel End Farm. Keep the stream, Wyth Burn, on the R, past waterfalls, Wythburn Head Tarns, and The Bog, to an old sheepfold at GR 296108, beyond Middle How. From near the sheepfold, cross the stream and ascend the slopes to the south-west, north of Flour Gill, to Greenup Edge. An alternative is to walk southwards to the hause at the head of Far Easedale, and then to ascend the path westwards to Greenup Edge. From the wide hause of Greenup Edge, follow Route 109 for the Langdale Pikes.

Route 112. Grasmere and Far Easedale. Leave Grasmere by the road, Easedale Road, going north-west. Continue along the road beyond a gate, and pass between houses to a stony track at GR 327085. (The path for the ascent of Helm Crag starts here.) Follow the path north-westwards, and cross Far Easedale Gill at Stythwaite Steps. The wild head of Far Easedale is now disclosed to the west and the path adhered to as far as the col on the skyline. This depression is often mistaken for Greenup Edge and is confusing in mist, because the stream beyond it is not Greenup Gill but descends through the Wythburn valley to Thirlmere. Therefore leave the stream on R, and advance on the path westwards to Greenup Edge on the low skyline ahead. On attaining the hause, turn L and follow Route 109 for the Langdale Pikes.

Route 113. By Easedale Tarn. Leave Grasmere by the road, Easedale Road, going north-west. At GR 331082, near a gate on the road, cross Easedale Beck, and follow the path towards the prominent white cascades of Sourmilk Gill. These are the key to Easedale Tarn, which lies in a great basin above them, dominated by Tarn Crag. Ascend the stony path to the foot of

Tarn Crag →

Langdale Pikes

Sergeant Man

Plate 200 **Route 113** passes this way

the tarn. Here there is the ruin of a former refreshment hut. Continue ahead, westwards, to the wild combe which may be identified by Blea Crag and Eagle Crag up on the L. An alternative path, less distinct, follows a route round the north side of Easedale Tarn. The two alternative paths merge below the zigzags and then the route passes to the L of the shapely little peak of Belles Knott. This reveals a beautiful retrospect of the blue sheet of water below. Codale Tarn soon appears on the R, on the approach to the crest of the ridge ahead. From this point, GR 292084, ascend the path on the interesting ridge to the cairn on Sergeant Man up on the hillside to the north-west. Either cross the moorland plateau to High Raise summit, or follow the path west. Thereafter follow the path over Thunacar Knott for Harrison Stickle.

Route 114. By Silver How. Leave Grasmere by the drive to Allen Bank, but when approaching the house diverge to R along a road which rises to Score Crag Farm. Follow the path westwards to the open fell, then south-west to Wray Gill. Then walk southwards for the grassy top of Silver How, 395 m, at GR 325066, which rises ahead. The cairn on this eminence reveals the route to the west in the direction of the Langdale Pikes. Follow the ridge path west, south of Lang How, then north-west via the col of Swinescar Hause to near Great Castle How, then west to the rocky ridge of Blea Rigg. From the path at GR 298080, descend on the path westwards to Stickle Tarn. Follow Route 104 or 105 to Harrison Stickle.

The chief attractions of this ascent are the vista from Silver How to the east over both Grasmere and Rydal Water, and the splendid prospect of the hills to the west round the head of Great Langdale.

Plate 201 The western prospect from Harrison Stickle

The Bowfell group

Bowfell	902 metres	2959 feet
Esk Pike	885 metres	2903 feet
Crinkle Crags	859 metres	2818 feet
Pike o'Blisco	705 metres	2313 feet
Cold Pike	701 metres	2300 feet
Esk Hause	*759 metres*	*2490 feet*
Wrynose Pass	*393 metres*	*1290 feet*

OS Map: Landranger 90 Penrith, Keswick & Ambleside
Outdoor Leisure 6 South Western Area

Bowfell

Route 115. Esk Hause and Esk Pike. Esk Pike rises to the south-east of Esk Hause, GR 233081, and the route to its summit is unmistakable on a good path. A short scramble detour from the path leads to the highest point, a rock outcrop. Note the precipitous front of Ill Crag to the west, above the head of Eskdale, and the view of Derwentwater to the north. The stygian surface of Angle Tarn, down on the east, is brought into view by walking a short way north from the summit outcrop. The long high ridge rising to Bowfell is disclosed to the south-east, but to reach it you must first descend the rough slopes to Ore Gap, and then either follow the path or follow the crest of the ridge (for views down into Mickleden) to the summit.

The panorama from Bowfell is very fine but does not live up to the expectations engendered by its shapely cone as seen from below. Skiddaw and Blencathra stand in splendid isolation on the northern horizon and the former is especially striking when observed under snow. It rises above Glaramara, which, however, obscures Derwentwater. The stony wastes of the Crinkles lie to the south, with the Coniston Fells overtopping them. Pike o'Blisco looks most graceful on L with Esthwaite Water and Windermere in the far distance.

The green pastures at the foot of Harter Fell are revealed to the R of Crinkle Crags, with the light glittering on Devoke Water away to the south-west. The Langdale Pikes are disappointing to the east and are backed by the Helvellyn and Fairfield ranges. The Scafell massif rises to the west beyond the vast solitudes of upper Eskdale, but this view of the group is not so fine as that from Long Top, on Crinkle Crags. Great Gable is in line with Great End while the Grasmoor range provides a ruddy skyline on their right.

Route 116. Rossett Gill and Ore Gap. From the Old Dungeon Ghyll Hotel, Great Langdale, follow Route 107 to the sheepfold, at GR 261073, situated near the end of Mickleden. Take the path on L which rises westwards near Rossett Gill, then zigzags to the left of the gill. On reaching the hause at the top of the gill, Angle Tarn is revealed in a rocky basin ahead with Hanging Knotts on L, and Rossett Pike on R. Keep to the Esk Hause path, but after passing the tarn bear to L, southwards, up the path to Ore Gap, and join Route 115 for Bowfell.

Note – Ore Gap was previously also known as Ure Gap or Ewer Gap.

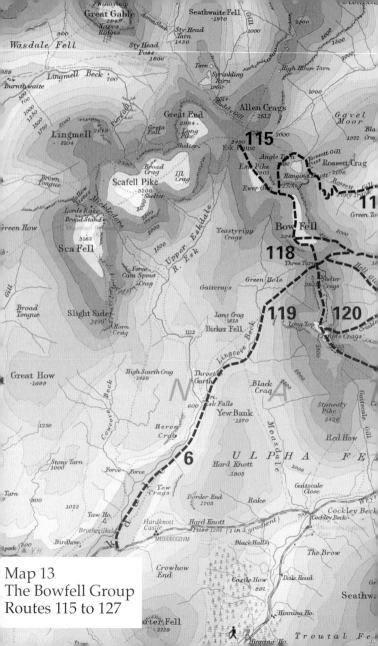

Map 13
The Bowfell Group
Routes 115 to 127

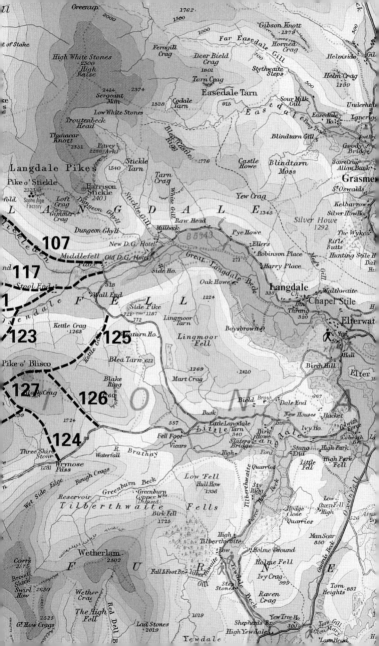

Route 117. By The Band direct. Pass through the gate at the road corner near the Old Dungeon Ghyll Hotel, and follow the farm road to Stool End. Go through the farmstead where a gate on L leads to the open fell. Scale the path rising straight ahead along The Band, and after crossing the marshy ground at its top, ascend the ridge immediately in front which rises to Bowfell. Note the fine outcrop of rock known as Bowfell Buttress on R, and on approaching the summit of the reigning peak diverge slightly to R to view the Great Slab, above Flat Crags, and Cambridge Crag beyond.

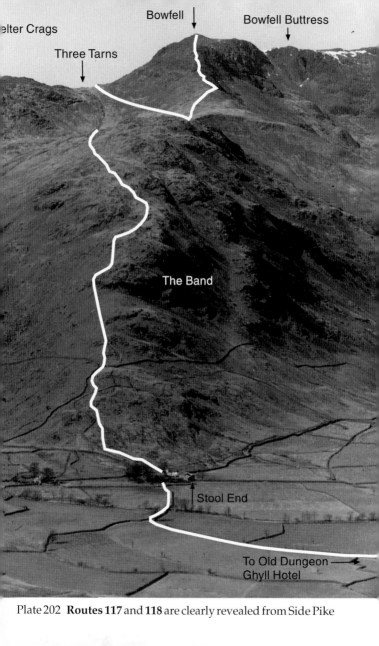

Bowfell

Bowfell Buttress

elter Crags

Three Tarns

The Band

Stool End

To Old Dungeon Ghyll Hotel

Plate 202 **Routes 117** and **118** are clearly revealed from Side Pike

Bowfell

To The Band

Shelter Crags

Three Tarns

Bowfell Links

To Lingcove

Pike O'Stickle

Gimmer Crag

The Great Slab

Plate 204 **Route 117** passes the Great Slab

Bowfell Buttress ←

Plate 206 **Route 118** passes Three Tarns

Plate 207 **Route 119** from Harter Fell

Route 118. By The Band and Three Tarns. Follow Route 117 as far as the marshy ground above The Band and then bear to L for the dip in the sky line. This discloses the pools known as Three Tarns some little distance ahead, then turn sharp to north, and ascend the steep path to the R of the crags of Bowfell Links. On reaching easier ground the path bears to the L, westwards, for the summit of Bowfell.

Route 119. Brotherilkeld and Lingcove Beck. This route starts from Brotherilkeld, near the foot of Hardknott Pass. Follow Route 6 as far as Lingcove Bridge, the packhorse bridge over Lingcove Beck, at GR 227036. Do not cross the bridge, but take the path on R of the beck and keep to it as far as Churn How, south of Green Hole. Make your way up the steep path north-eastwards, where Bowfell towers overhead on L, to Three Tarns, and pick up Route 118 for the summit of the mountain.

Crinkle Crags

Route 120. From Three Tarns. Reach Three Tarns either by Route 118, from Great Langdale, or by Route 119 from Brotherilkeld. Proceed southwards on the path from the hause of Three Tarns, and make your way through the maze of Shelter Crags as a prelude to the traverse of the more lofty ridge of the Crinkles. Keep well on L near the edge overlooking Great Langdale to scan the many rifts on its eastern front, and to observe with delight the winding course of the great valley at your feet. Note especially the impressive Mickle Door on L immediately below Long Top, for it discloses an attractive aspect of Pike o'Blisco across Browney Gill far below, and is the exit usually used by those who have ascended near Crinkle Gill. Long Top, at 859 m, is Crinkle Crags' summit.

There are two conspicious features in the panorama from Long Top which are worthy of special mention. The prospect of the 'Lakeland Giants' is most revealing, for the two Scafells are clearly delineated to the north-west, and particularly so the topography of the more westerly peak. The rift enclosing Cam Spout is well seen, as also the depression above it which terminates in the gap of Mickledore. In addition to this spectacle of wild mountain grandeur, Bowfell discloses its real majesty to the north with Skiddaw peeping over its right shoulder. Moreover the gullies of rotten rock known as Bowfell Links are clearly perceived seaming its southern façade high above one of the greatest stony wildernesses in Lakeland.

Route 121. By Hell Gill. Follow Route 117 to Stool End. Go through the farmstead where a gate on L leads to the open fell. Pass the path to The Band on R and follow the path towards Oxendale Beck. Pass a sheepfold and continue along the path west over rough ground to the footbridge at GR 263052. An easier, and safer, final approach to the footbridge is to use the path variation higher up the hillside on R, after leaving the stone wall behind on R.

Cross the footbridge, and ascend the steep path south of the beck. The waterfall of Whorneyside Force is passed, before you cross the beck at the bottom of the ravine of Hell Gill. Ascend the well-made path to the L of the ravine, before continuing ahead on a grassy path near Buscoe Sike. On reaching the hause of Three Tarns turn sharp L, and follow Route 120, south, for Crinkle Crags.

Route 122. By Crinkle Gill. Follow Route 121 as far as the footbridge at GR 263052; cross it and walk L to the wild rocky exit of Crinkle Gill. There are two alternatives for this route by Crinkle Gill: a scramble ascent in the ravine itself, or an ascent alongside, north of it.

Enter the gill only when the stream is not in spate. A scramble ascent may be made with care, to include a narrow first section, left bend, a staircase by cascades, a walk in a wide gorge and under a flying buttress of rock, to a final deeply enclosed basin or amphitheatre, where several streamlets come

Mickle Door

Plate 208 **Route 120** opens up a fine view of Pike o' Blisco

Shelter Crags

Plate 210 **Route 121** passes the fall of Whorneyside Force

Plate 211 **Route 121** goes up beside Hell Gill

together. Escape from the amphitheatre via a gully left of the second stream, and then via a path above the first (left-hand) cascade. There is a little 'saddleback' feature, at height about 550 m, above the amphitheatre.

If the above scramble is not followed, then an ascent from the exit of Crinkle Gill can be made westwards, north of the gill on rocky ground and terraces, overlooking the ravine, to height approx. 550 m, above the amphitheatre, at GR 254049.

From this point ascend the rough ground westwards. There is a prominent cairn on a boulder, below the scree of Mickle Door now towering overhead. Scramble up the scree bed to gain the skyline and then turn L for the highest Crinkle and later R to set foot on Long Top.

Note – An interesting alternative direct ascent from Oxendale is as follows, starting from the path to Hell Gill. After attaining the top of the first rise, it takes a line for the ridge west, first over grass and then through scattered boulders to the base of the long stone shoot which slants R up to the skyline. From the ridge so reached, north of Gunson Knott, follow the ridge path south for Crinkle Crags summit.

Route 123. By Browney Gill. This stream is deeply enclosed on both sides; the path keeps well away from it until its higher reaches are attained. Follow Route 121 to the sheepfold near Oxendale Beck, and cross the stream here. On the other side pick up the path that slants diagonally uphill to a depression, near Brown Howe, well up the flanks of Pike o'Blisco, and continue high above Browney Gill, on R, until close to Red Tarn. Do not go as far as the tarn, but cross the stream near its outflow and then take the path following an oblique course across the lower slopes of Cold Pike, keeping a wild ravine on R. On reaching easier ground, use the path to make for the skyline to the north-west, at the first Crinkle. During the latter part of the ascent there are magnificent views R into the savage recesses of Crinkle Gill. From the top of the first Crinkle so reached, there is a grassy depression to be crossed before the ascent to the summit of Crinkle Crags. For this final ascent to the summit, either ascend directly the rocky gully ahead, which includes an awkward rock scramble known as The Bad Step, or use a grassy rake to the L (west) of this, to avoid the difficulty.

Note – An alternative is to follow Route 121 to the footbridge at GR 263052. Cross it then proceed south, across Crinkle Gill, to near Isaac Gill. The ravine of Browney Gill rises ahead. Ascend the slopes south-west on the tongue between Isaac Gill and Crinkle Gill. A short detour can be made to view the rocky pinnacle of Gladstone's Finger, near Gladstone Knott, GR 256046. Ascend the rocky slopes south-west then south to the top of Gladstone Knott. On attaining the higher ground, skirt the rim of Great Cove to join the path near the base of the first Crinkle.

Route 124. Wrynose Pass and Cold Pike. Take the path going in a north-westerly direction from the Three Shires Stone, near the top of Wrynose Pass. At GR 271036, on Redtarn Moss, cross the marshy ground south-west, on path traces, south of a pool, south of Red Tarn. Follow a path south-west on to the ridge, then turn R, north-west, for Cold Pike summit, with its three tops, which is the southern sentinel of the Crinkles. Then proceed in a north-westerly direction, across a broad grassy depression, to pick up the path of Route 123 near Great Knott, for Crinkle Crags.

Plate 212 **Routes 122, 123** and **124** to Crinkle Crags

Pike o' Blisco

Coniston Fells

Red Tarn

Browney
Gill

Crinkle Gil

The Band

Plate 213 **Route 123** and alternative

Oxendale Sheep Fold

Plate 214 **Route 123** from Oxendale

Cold Pike

Track To Crinkle Crags →

Browney Gill →

Red Tarn ←

...217 Route 192 is very popular with fell walkers

Plate 216 The Lakeland Giants from the Crinkles

Scafell Pike

Mickledore

Scafell

Long Top

Cam Spout Crag

Upper Eskdale

Pike o'Blisco

Route 125. Langdale and Redacre Gill. Start at the steep section of the road at GR 286052, south-east of Wall End. Walk up a path through the bracken on R. Pick up Redacre Gill and follow the path on its R, to near its source, keeping Kettle Crag well on R. Then bear westwards and ascend the final rocky slopes of Pike o'Blisco. The summit consists of a rocky platform crowned by a large cairn, and commands a grand prospect of Great Langdale, as well as one of the most impressive aspects of the shattered front of Crinkle Crags.

Route 126. Little Langdale and Fell Foot. Fell Foot is the last farm in Little Langdale and stands at the bottom of Wrynose Pass just short of its junction with the road going over to Blea Tarn and Great Langdale. Ascend the pass as far as Wrynose Bridge, and then turn off to R beyond it to pick up the path traces, with some small well-placed cairns, heading north-westwards. This joins Route 124, at height about 640 m, east of Pike o'Blisco summit.

Route 127. From Red Tarn. Reach Red Tarn either by following Route 123 from Oxendale, or by the path from the Three Shires Stone, Wrynose Pass summit. From the paths crossroads at GR 267039, turn up the fellside north-east following the path to the summit of Pike o'Blisco.

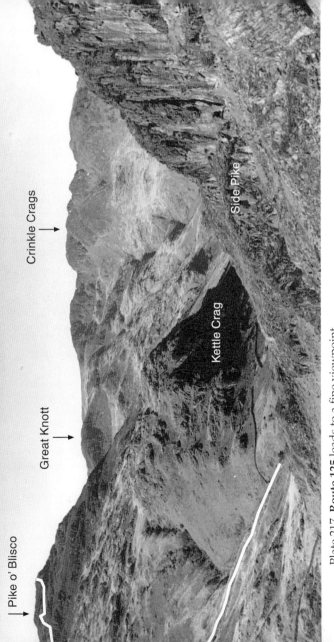

Plate 217 **Route 125** leads to a fine viewpoint

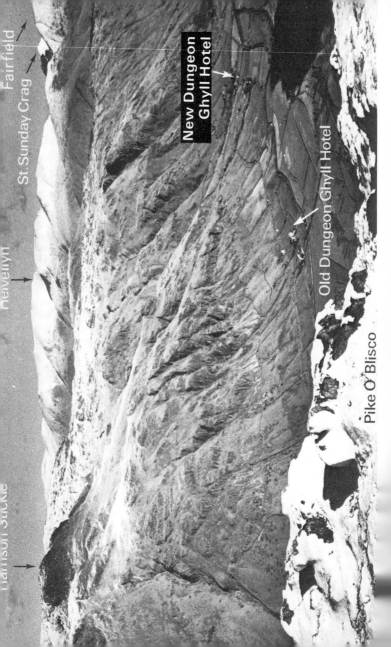

Fairfield

St Sunday Crag

Helvellyn

Harrison Stickle

New Dungeon Ghyll Hotel

Old Dungeon Ghyll Hotel

Pike O'Blisco

The Coniston group and Harter Fell, Eskdale

Old Man	803 metres	2634 feet
Swirl How	802 metres	2631 feet
Brim Fell	796 metres	2611 feet
Great Carrs	785 metres	2575 feet
Dow Crag	778 metres	2552 feet
Grey Friar	c773 metres	2536 feet
Wetherlam	762 metres	2500 feet
Harter Fell	653 metres	2142 feet
Border End	522 metres	1712 feet
Hardknott Pass	*393 metres*	*1290 feet*
Wrynose Pass	*393 metres*	*1290 feet*

OS Map: Landranger 90 Penrith, Keswick & Ambleside
Landranger 96 Barrow-in-Furness & South Lakeland
Outdoor Leisure 6 South Wstern Area

Coniston Old Man

Route 128. By the quarries. This is the shortest, least interesting but most popular ascent of the mountain. Leave Coniston by the turning on L of the Sun Hotel and follow the track across a field near Dixon Ground and over a bridge when Church Beck appears on R. Ascend the path beside the beck, to Miners Bridge. Do not cross the bridge. Instead follow the path that sweeps round the hillside west, and the summit of the Old Man is revealed to the west. Advance towards it, to a junction, at GR 285981, with the old quarry road coming in on the L from the car-park at 'Fell Gate', at GR 289970. Note that this car-park provides an alternative starting point for the walk; from the car-park walk along the old quarry road, to the L of The Bell, to the path/quarry road junction mentioned above. To pass through the workings below Low Water, follow the old quarry

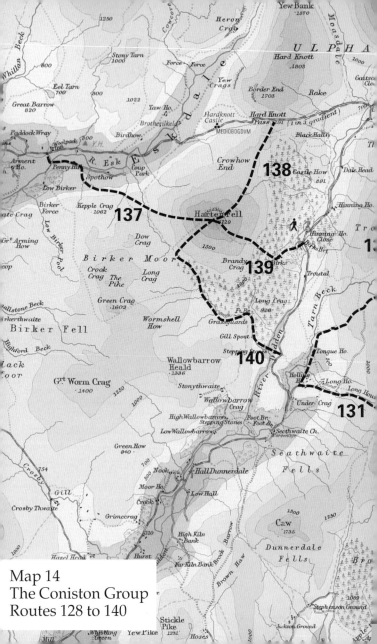

Map 14
The Coniston Group
Routes 128 to 140

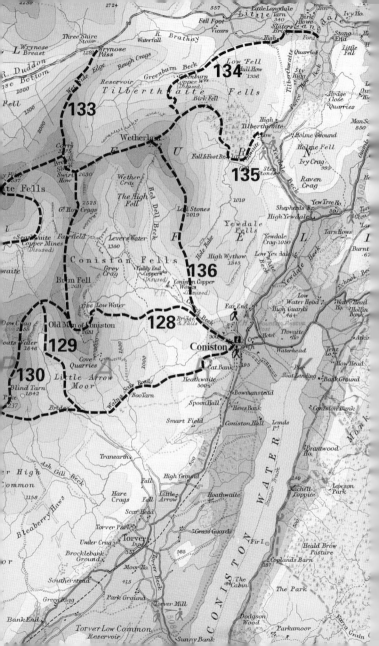

road, which ultimately discloses the tarn in a wild setting. Skirt its south side and ascend the zigzags which rise to the ridge leading to the R for the cairn on the summit of the mountain.

This route may be varied by taking the uphill road for Coppermines Valley just north of the bridge in the village. It swings round to L to reach Church Beck at Miners Bridge. The previous route may be reached by crossing the bridge.

The panorama from the Old Man is famous for its extensive prospects to the south and east, where the patterned fields and wooded knolls stretch away to the sea in the dim distance. The most conspicuous feature in this vast landscape is Coniston Water, which is revealed completely far below. There are also glimpses of Tarn Hows and two sections of Windermere to the east, while the sands of the Duddon gleam far away in the south-west, to L of the great whaleback of Black Combe. The view round the rest of the arc contrasts strangely with this sylvan scene, for it reveals a confused mass of mountains without disclosing a single peak in its entirety. The summit of Dow Crag lies to the west, but to see Goat's Water at its base it is necessary to descend some distance below the cairn. The Scafells appear to the north-west above the rounded top of Grey Friar, while Skiddaw, Blencathra and the Helvellyn range rise above Brim Fell and Wetherlam to the north. The long line of hills dominated by High Street are seen to the north-east and terminate in the south with the columnar beacon of Thornthwaite Crag and the graceful cone of Ill Bell.

Plate 219 Dow Crag and Coniston Old Man from Torver

Route 129. By Goat's Water. Leave Coniston by the road rising to the old railway station, then ascend the steep road ahead, south-west. This rises to the open fell at 'Fell Gate', and then bends to R for the quarries on the eastern face of the Old Man. Note that cars may be left at the car-park at GR 289970. Take the grassy Walna Scar Road which undulates over the open fell at the base of the reigning peak, passes the reedy pool known as Boo Tarn, and then rises through two rock gateways with Brown Pike dominating the skyline to the west. At GR 274965 turn sharp to R across the moor and follow the grassy path into The Cove, whence the stony path is seen bending to L to enter the wild combe at the base of Dow Crag. On rounding the escarpment on R, Goat's Water appears immediately ahead. Keep it on L and make for the dip, Goat's Hawse, in the skyline to the north. On attaining this grassy col, bear sharp to R, and ascend the path east then south-east for the cairn on the Old Man. During the latter part of the ascent the five magnificent rock buttresses of Dow Crag frown upon the vast scree slopes and the black waters of the tarn at their base. They are one of the most important climbing grounds in Lakeland and beloved by the expert cragsman.

Route 130. Walna Scar and Brown Pike. Follow Route 129 to beyond the rock gateways on the Walna Scar Road. Continue along the road in the direction of Brown Pike, passing over Cove Bridge, at GR 270965, which reveals the zigzags of the track to the west; ascend the track until the col of the Walna Scar pass is attained. The top of Walna Scar fell may be reached by a short detour south-west. On reaching the pass, the view bursting upon the eye to the west is one of the surprises of this route. It discloses not only the Duddon valley below but also the long line of hills stretching from Black Combe on L to the shapely peak of Harter Fell on R. The Scafells rise on the northern horizon. Now turn sharp to R and ascend the grassy slopes of Brown Pike, whose cairn reveals a fine prospect to

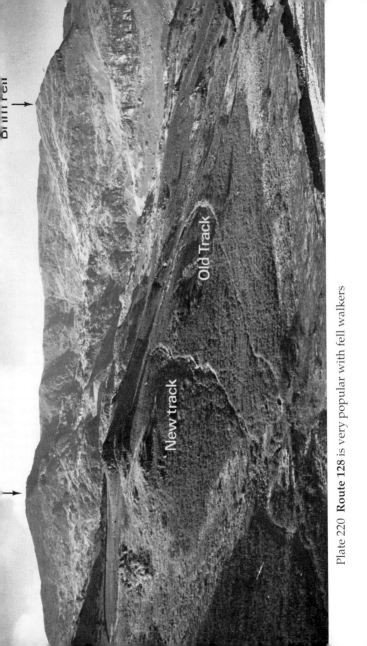

Plate 220 **Route 128** is very popular with fell walkers

Slight Side | Scafell | Mickledore | Crag | Ill Crag | Great End | Pike | Bowfell | Brim Fell

Plate 222 The vast north-western prospect from the summit of the Old Man

Walna Scar Road

Quartz Cairn

Goats Water

Track to Goats Water

Plate 224 **Route 129**—Dow Crag is first unveiled from this cairn

Plate 225 **Route 129**—Dow Crag from Goat's Water

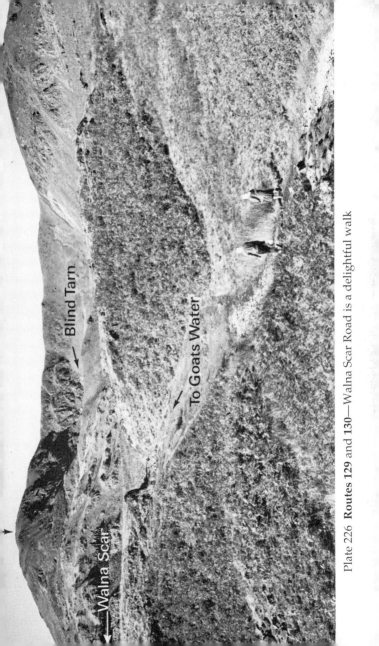

Walna Scar

Blind Tarn

To Goats Water

Plate 226 **Routes 129** and **130**—Walna Scar Road is a delightful walk

Goat's Water

Dow Crag

Buck Pike

To Coniston

To Walna Scar

Plate 228 **Route 130** is the only walk that reveals Blind Tarn

Blind Tarn

Plate 230 **Route 130** yields a close view of the precipices of
Dow Crag

the east and south which is not dissimilar to that seen from the Old Man. Walk northwards along the crest of the ridge to Buck Pike, noting the almost perfect circle of Blind Tarn below on R. On reaching Buck Pike observe the splendour of the view which encompasses the Scafells, Dow Crag, and Coniston Old Man on the other side of Goat's Water, far below. Now walk along the ridge and ascend the final slopes of Dow Crag, meanwhile noting the great yawning gullies on R which form the savage recesses of this magnificent crag. Scramble carefully over the rocky summit and while descending the rough rocky ridge to Goat's Hawse note the fine conical form of Harter Fell on L. At the col join Route 129 for the summit of Coniston Old Man.

Route 131. Seathwaite and Walna Scar. Leave the hamlet by the road heading north and keep Tarn Beck on L until Seathwaite Bridge appears ahead. Here, at GR 232968, the road forks; take the right branch and follow it close to Long House to Long House Gill. The road bifurcates again, with the left branch rising to Seathwaite Tarn. Take the stony track on R, which goes up the fellside to the east. Leave some unsightly quarry workings on R and gain the grassy track which bends round to L and rises across the flanks of Walna Scar fell. On reaching the pass, ascend Brown Pike on L and follow Route 130 for Dow Crag and the Old Man.

Route 132. Seathwaite and Grey Friar. From Seathwaite take Route 131 as far as High Holling House, at GR 235969. Take the farm road past Low Holling House to Tongue House. Follow Tarn Beck for a short distance north, but then turn to R and ascend the path north-eastwards, to reach the road for Seathwaite Tarn reservoir. Follow the road to the dam at the tarn. Pass round the western shore of the tarn, to the disused mine workings east of its head. Walk up the valley of Tarn

Head Beck, northwards, before attacking the final slopes of Grey Friar west-north-west then north, over rough ground.

A more direct route, from near the outlet of Seathwaite Tarn, is to ascend Tarn Brow, north-north-east, to gain the ridge of Troutal Fell. From here ascend the slopes north-east to the summit of Grey Friar.

The prospect to the north-west from this outpost of the Coniston Fells is incredibly beautiful and one of the most impressive in Lakeland. The fine serrated skyline of the Scafell group rises above the wild recesses of upper Eskdale, and the eye is irresistibly led towards them over the wastes of Mosedale far below, between the craggy, hummocked top of Hard Knott on L and the declivities of Little Stand on R. Cockley Beck and Wrynose Bottom are hidden by the slopes of Grey Friar in the foreground but the symmetrical cone of Harter Fell is well seen in isolation to the west.

Now turn your steps north-eastwards and descend to the broad col of Fairfield. From here, either swing round to the south-east to gain the ridge near Great How Crags, or, with little extra effort, visit Great Carrs summit and Swirl How summit for the ridge to Great How Crags. This top overlooks Levers Water, and also discloses the long whaleback ridge of Brim Fell to the south which terminates with the Old Man. Walk along its undulations to attain the cairn on the reigning peak.

Bowfell

Long Top

Little Stand

Seathwaite Reservoir

To Walna Scar

Tongue House

Plate 232 **Route 132**—The Scafell Pikes from Grey Friar

Swirl How

Route 133. Wrynose Pass, Great Carrs and Swirl How. From Wrynose Pass summit ascend the path south-westwards, with a final zigzag east then south to the ridge, close to (west of) a prominent cairn. A less distinct path variation leaves this path at a height about 480 m to make a direct line for the cairn. From this point, GR 274021, on Wet Side Edge continue along the well-worn path over Little Carrs to Great Carrs, which is the northern sentinel of the range. Energetic fell walkers may prefer to keep to the edge of the precipices on the L, surmounting the several craggy satellites *en route*.

The cairn discloses a wide panorama of fell and dale with Pike o'Blisco to the north and the Crinkles on its left. These are overtopped by Bowfell, which merges with the Scafells in the north-west, while the Helvellyn range rises on the north-eastern horizon well above the intervening moorland. The most attractive vista, however, is to the east, where Greenburn Tarn is cradled in the vast combe far below, with the light reflected by Little Langdale Tarn beyond it, and the Fairfield range forming a great barrier across the skyline in the background.

Walk southwards round the shattered rim of Broad Slack and ascend east to the cairn on Swirl How, another fine viewpoint, then continue along the ridge to Great How Crags and Brim Fell for the Old Man of Coniston.

Those coming from Fell Foot should ascend the path into the Greenburn valley and then ascend the ridge of Wet Side Edge direct.

Plate 233 **Route 133** reveals the length of *Wet Side Edge*

Prison Band →   Swirl How →   Great Carrs →

Plate 235 **Route 133**—Greenburn Tarn from Great Carrs

Wetherlam

Route 134. Little Langdale and Wetherlam. From the road junction at GR 316034, Little Langdale, go downhill by the road leading to the ford across the River Brathay. Follow the track west, with Slater or Slater's Bridge, and Little Langdale Tarn, on R, to beyond Low Hall Garth. At the junction at GR 305028, bear to L on a path over the lower slopes of Low Fell into the Greenburn valley. (*Note* – The other track at the junction provides an approach from Fell Foot Bridge.) When the disused Greenburn Mine workings are reached, east of the reservoir of Greenburn Tarn, turn to L and walk up the zigzag path southwards to Birk Fell Hawse. Ascend the craggy flanks of Wetherlam Edge to the south-west until the cairn on Wetherlam summit is attained.

The view round the northern arc is superb and includes the Scafells, the Crinkles and Bowfell, the Langdale Pikes and the Helvellyn range. The Langdale Pikes, however, present a disappointing aspect owing to their lower elevation and appear much more impressive from the ridge lower down above Birk Fell. The vista to the east also is magnificent, for it reveals the flatter, green country towards Windermere, and includes Coniston Water, Tarn Hows and Esthwaite Water.

Descend westwards from the summit, over the shoulder of Black Sails, until Swirl Hawse is reached, noting that Levers Water is down on the left. Scramble up the rocky ridge of Prison Band to the top of Swirl How. Follow the ridge southwards, to Great How Crags and Brim Fell, for the Old Man of Coniston.

Route 135. Tilberthwaite Gill and Wetherlam. This wild and picturesque ravine is one of the favourite venues of the Lakeland visitor. From the car-park at GR 306010, near Low Tilberthwaite, the path at GR 300008, near the head of the ravine, may be reached by ascending either side of it as follows:

1. Take the path south-west, past some large old quarries and continue on the path westwards, which reveals good views of Yewdale Beck in the ravine low down on R. This path eventually crosses Crook Beck and turns R across the gill above the ravine at a footbridge to reach the path at GR 300008.

Or: 2. Cross the bridge from the car-park and go R of Low Tilberthwaite to reach the quarry road behind the house. Walk along this gradually rising course, with the gill low down on R until it turns round to the R, north, near the head of the ravine.

Wetherlam now towers overhead, to the west, but the easiest approach is by the rough track north which ends below and to the south of Birk Fell. From here walk up the fellside north-west to the path at Birk Fell Hawse. Now ascend Wetherlam Edge for the summit of Wetherlam, and follow Route 134 for Swirl How and the Old Man of Coniston

Route 136. Coniston and Wetherlam. From Coniston reach Miners Bridge either by the path from near the Sun Hotel or by the road for Coppermines Valley; see Route 128. Follow the Coppermines Valley road for a short distance and then take the path on R which rises gently across the hillside northwards to the hawse of Hole Rake. Ascend the slopes north-west for the ridge of Lad Stones. Proceed over its many tops until the cairn on Wetherlam is attained, noting the fine views on L of Great How Crags and Swirl How. The fell in the foreground of this view is the ridge coming down south from Black Sails. This provides an alternative approach to Wetherlam as follows. From Miners Bridge follow the Coppermines Valley road and track to the foot of Levers Water. Ascend the fellside east on to the ridge then walk up the ridge north to Black Sails from where Wetherlam top is reached across marsh.

From Wetherlam summit follow Route 134 for Swirl How and the Old Man of Coniston.

Coniston Old Man → Lad Stones → Little Langdale → Great Carrs → Wet Side Edge → Wrynose Pass →

Plate 237 **Route 134** as seen from near Skelwith Bridge

Pike o' Stickle | Loft Crag | Harrison Stickle | Pavey Ark | Sergeant Man | Lingmoor

Side Pike

Blea Tarn

Wetherlam

Plate 239 **Routes 135 and 136**—Wetherlam and Yewdale

Wetherlam

Plate 240 **Route 135**—Tilberthwaite Gill

Wetherlam

Plate 241 **Route 136**—Coppermines Valley

Fairfield

Lad Stones
& Wetherlam

Plate 243 **Route 136**—Western prospect from Lad Stones

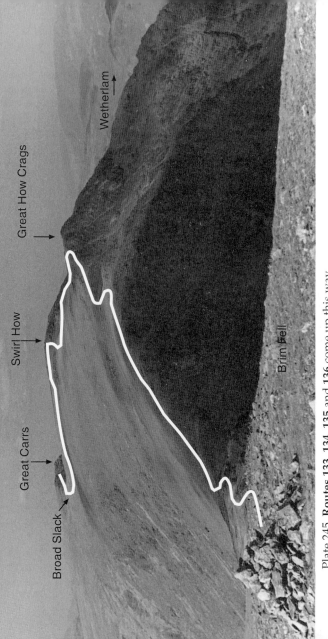

Plate 245 **Routes 133, 134, 135 and 136** come up this way

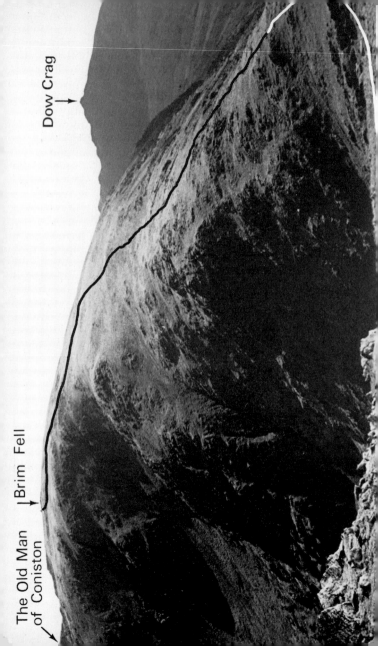

The Old Man
of Coniston

↓Brim Fell

Dow Crag

Harter Fell, Eskdale

Route 137. Eskdale and Penny Hill. Leave the Eskdale highway by the road at GR 189009 near the Woolpack Inn. Cross Doctor Bridge which spans the River Esk and follow the farm road to Penny Hill Farm. Pass through the farmstead and bear to R on a track which rises gently south-eastwards. From a height about 160 m, at GR 198003, beyond a sheepfold, ascend a path south then turn sharp L and follow a stone wall as it contours almost level across the craggy hillside, to an unnamed stream. Now make your way south-east on a path through an obvious wide gap in the crags. There is a prominent perched boulder overhead, to the left. Proceed further, to cross Spothow Gill above its ravine, and to reach a stile at a fence at GR 207000. Follow the path eastwards. Thereafter your route is clear as it rises across the open fell and skirts the collection of massive crags on L before attaining the three conspicuous rocky cones that crown the summit of the mountain. These afford some easy scrambling and their tops cannot be reached without the use of hands. This route is the most interesting and revealing ascent of Harter Fell, because as height is gained all the 'Lakeland Giants' appear one by one on L across Eskdale, whereas the route which starts from the foot of Hardknott Pass, at Jubilee Bridge, has all the views behind the walker, with the only compensation of the vista along Eskdale on the R. This latter route joins the route from Penny Hill Farm at GR 208000.

The splendid isolation of the summit of Harter Fell opens up a panorama in all directions and includes the green straths of both Eskdale and the Duddon valley together with the massive group of hills dominated by the Old Man of Coniston. It is the vista to the north, however, that will hold your gaze, for the Scafells rise superbly above upper Eskdale and form a magnificent skyline which merges on R with Bowfell and the Crinkles, while the thin line of the road rising to Hardknott Pass threads the valley at your feet.

Route 138. From Hardknott Pass. Proceed southwards from the crest of the pass and pick up the path to the summit of Harter Fell, traversing the slopes east of Demming Crag. There are fine views of the Duddon valley on L.

Note – **Border End** is the rocky shoulder of Hard Knott fell overlooking Hardknott Roman Fort and Pass. Its summit unveils the most dramatic view of the 'Lakeland Giants', from Scafell to Bowfell. To attain it all you have to do is to use the path north from the summit of the pass and then ascend the rocky ground north-west. This diversion is one of the most rewarding in all Lakeland. See Plate 3.

Route 139. From Birks Bridge. From Birks Bridge, at GR 234993, follow the track through Great Wood to Birks. Ascend the rough road west, then ascend the path west in the forest, near a gill to the open fell. Follow the path north-west to the summit of Harter Fell.

Route 140. Seathwaite and Grassguards. From the road at GR 231975 north of Seathwaite, descend the path westwards to the stepping stones, Fickle Steps, at the River Duddon. Cross the stones and walk up the path to the footbridge at Grass-guards, keeping the stream on L all the way. Cross the bridge and take the path west then north-west. The path then crosses the gill and heads north-west to reach the open fell at GR 211992. From this point take the path ascending north-eastwards. This joins with the path of Route 137 coming in from L, a short distance west of the summit of Harter Fell.

Plate 247 Harter Fell is reached by **Route 137** and variation

Grassguards

Penny Hill

Harter Fell

Wha House

Hardknott Pass

To
Harter Fell
←

Plate 249 **Route 139**—Birks Bridge. The pools below are a favourite with bathers

Birks Bridge

To Seathwaite

Harter Fell

To Cockley Beck

Grassguards

This **Route Card** is now in use in Scotland and Snowdonia; the idea is sound and if adopted and used consistently by all climbers and walkers throughout our mountainous country it could be the means of facilitating any call for Mountain Rescue. It is, of course, most important that **no digression** is made from the stated route, otherwise in the even of an accident searchers would be unable to locate the victim.

Leave word
when you go
on our hills

Names and Addresses: Home Address and Local Address	Route
Time and date of departure	Bad weather alternative
Place of Departure and registered number of vehicle (if any)	
Estimated time of return	Walking/Climbing (delete as necessary)

GO UP WELL EQUIPPED — TO COME BACK SAFELY

Please tick items carried

Emergency Food	Torch	Ice Axe
Waterproof Clothing (colour:	Whistle	Crampons
	Map	Polybag
Winter Clothing (colour:	Compass	First Aid

Please complete and leave with landlady, warden etc.
Ask landlady or warden to contact Police if you are overdue
PLEASE REPORT YOUR SAFE RETURN

An Appeal from Mountain Rescue Teams

FELL WALKERS!
READ THIS

and live a little longer ...

British mountains can be killers if proper care is not taken. The following notes cover the <u>minimum</u> precautions if you want to avoid getting hurt or lost, and so inconveniencing or endangering others as well as yourselves.

CLOTHING. This should be colourful, warm, windproof and waterproof. Wear boots with nails or moulded rubber soles, <u>not</u> shoes, plimsolls, or gum-boots. Take a woollen cap and a spare jersey; it is always colder on the tops.

FOOD. <u>In addition to</u> the usual sandwiches take chocolate, dates, mint cake or similar sweet things which restore energy quickly. If you don't need them yourself, someone else may.

EQUIPMENT. This <u>must</u> include map, compass, and at least one reliable watch in the party. A whistle and torch (a series of six blasts or flashes repeated at minute intervals signal an emergency) and, in winter conditions, an ice-axe and survival bag are <u>essential.</u>

COMPANY. Don't go alone, and make sure party leaders are experienced. Take special care of the youngest and weakest in dangerous places.

EMERGENCIES. Don't press on if conditions are against you — turn back even if it upsets your plan. Learn a little first aid, and keep injured or exhausted people warm until help reaches you. Get a message to the Police for help as soon as possible, and report changes of route or time-table to them if someone is expecting you. The Police will do the rest.

This is a copy of the leaflet published and distributed free of charge by the Lake District Mountain Accidents Association with the help of voluntary donations from the public.

DANGERS WHICH CAN ALWAYS BE AVOIDED—
and should be, until you know how to cope with
them:

Precipices
    Slopes of ice,
        or steep snow,
            or very steep grass (especially frozen),
                or unstable boulders.
Gullies and stream beds.
    Streams in spate.
        Snow cornices on ridges or gully tops.
            Over-ambition.
                Plain damned carelessness.

DANGERS WHICH MAY SURPRISE YOU—
and should be guarded against:

Weather changes -- mist, gale, rain or snow.
  Get forecasts, and watch the sky.

Ice on paths.
  Carry an ice-axe.

Excessive cold or heat.
  Dress sensibly, and take a spare jersey.

Incipient exhaustion.
  Know the signs; rest and keep warm.

Accident or illness.
  **Don't panic. If you send for help, make sure that
  the rescuers know exactly where to come.**

Flight of time.
  Learn your own pace. Plan your walk.

It is no disgrace to turn back if you are not certain.
A party must be governed by the capabilities of the
weakest member.

THINGS TO THINK OF BEFORE YOU SET OUT

Can you use map and compass in mist or storm?
(Be prepared before you're caught).

Do you know the safe ways off in emergency? (If the map
doesn't tell you, ask someone who does know.)

How will you keep the party together? (Stragglers may
mean trouble and danger to yourselves and others.)

Who knows where you are going and when you should be
back? (If you come down somewhere else, send word at
once, or get in touch with the Police.)

ENJOY YOURSELVES, BUT DON'T PLAY THE FOOL

Index